D0150792

Lab Manual for Statistical Analysis

Sara Miller McCune founded SAGE Publishing in 1965 to support the dissemination of usable knowledge and educate a global community. SAGE publishes more than 1000 journals and over 800 new books each year, spanning a wide range of subject areas. Our growing selection of library products includes archives, data, case studies and video. SAGE remains majority owned by our founder and after her lifetime will become owned by a charitable trust that secures the company's continued independence.

Los Angeles | London | New Delhi | Singapore | Washington DC | Melbourne

Lab Manual for Statistical Analysis

Dawn M. McBride
Illinois State University

J. Cooper Cutting
Illinois State University

Los Angeles | London | New Delhi
Singapore | Washington DC | Melbourne

FOR INFORMATION:

SAGE Publications, Inc.
2455 Teller Road
Thousand Oaks, California 91320
E-mail: order@sagepub.com

SAGE Publications Ltd.
1 Oliver's Yard
55 City Road
London EC1Y 1SP
United Kingdom

SAGE Publications India Pvt. Ltd.
B 1/I 1 Mohan Cooperative Industrial Area
Mathura Road, New Delhi 110 044
India

SAGE Publications Asia-Pacific Pte. Ltd.
3 Church Street
#10-04 Samsung Hub
Singapore 049483

Acquisitions Editor: Abbie Rickard
Content Development Editor: Morgan Shannon
Editorial Assistant: Jennifer Cline
Production Editor: Olivia Weber-Stenis
Copy Editor: Erin Livingston
Typesetter: C&M Digitals (P) Ltd.
Proofreader: Jeff Bryant
Cover Designer: Scott Van Atta
Marketing Manager: Jenna Retana

Copyright © 2018 by SAGE Publications, Inc.

All rights reserved. No part of this book may be reproduced or utilized in any form or by any means, electronic or mechanical, including photocopying, recording, or by any information storage and retrieval system, without permission in writing from the publisher.

All trademarks depicted within this book, including trademarks appearing as part of a screenshot, figure, or other image are included solely for the purpose of illustration and are the property of their respective holders. The use of the trademarks in no way indicates any relationship with, or endorsement by, the holders of said trademarks. SPSS is a registered trademark of International Business Machines Corporation. Excel is a registered trademark of Microsoft Corporation.

Printed in the United States of America

ISBN 978-1-5063-2517-0

This book is printed on acid-free paper.

17 18 19 20 21 10 9 8 7 6 5 4 3 2 1

Contents

Preface   viii

Introduction for Students   ix

Section 1. Topic Activities   1

    1. Statistics in the Media   2

    2. The Purpose of Statistics   3

    3. Understanding Your Data   4

    4. Research Concepts: Designs, Validity, and Scales of Measurement   5

    5. Measurement Group Activity   6

    6. Designing an Experiment Group Activity   7

    7. Experimental Variables   8

    8. Distributions and Probability   9

    9. Displaying Distributions   10

    10. Setting Up Your Data in SPSS: Creating a Data File   11

    11. Displaying Distributions in SPSS   12

    12. Basic Probability   13

    13. Sampling   14

    14. Central Tendency 1   15

    15. Central Tendency 2   16

    16. Central Tendency in SPSS   17

    17. Describing a Distribution by Hand   18

    18. More Describing Distributions   19

    19. Descriptive Statistics Exercise   20

    20. Descriptive Statistics With Excel   22

    21. Measures of Variability in SPSS   23

    22. Calculating z Scores Using SPSS   24

    23. The Normal Distribution   25

    24. z Scores and the Normal Distribution   26

    25. Hypothesis Testing With Normal Populations   27

    26. Stating Hypotheses and Choosing Tests   28

    27. Hypothesis Testing With z Tests   30

    28. Hypothesis Testing With a Single Sample   31

    29. One-Sample t Test in SPSS   32

    30. One-Sample t Tests by Hand   33

    31. Related Samples t Tests   34

    32. Related Samples t Test in SPSS   36

    33. Independent Samples t Tests   37

34. Hypothesis Testing: Multiple Tests — 38
35. More Hypothesis Tests With Multiple Tests — 40
36. *t* Tests Summary Worksheet — 43
37. Choose the Correct *t* Test — 44
38. One-Way Between-Subjects ANOVA by Hand — 46
39. One-Way Between-Subjects ANOVA in SPSS — 47
40. Factorial ANOVA — 48
41. One-Way Within-Subjects ANOVA — 51
42. One-Way Within-Subjects ANOVA in SPSS — 52
43. ANOVA Review — 54
44. Which Test Should I Use? — 56
45. Correlations and Scatterplots Exercise — 58
46. Correlations and Scatterplots 2 — 59
47. Correlations and Scatterplots in SPSS — 60
48. Computing Correlations by Hand — 61
49. Computing Correlations by Hand 2 — 62
50. Hypothesis Testing With Correlation — 63
51. Hypothesis Testing With Correlation Using SPSS — 64
52. Regression — 65
53. Chi-Square Test for Independence — 66

Section 2. Meet the Formulae — 67
54. Meet the Formula: Standard Deviation — 68
55. Meet the Formula: *z* Score Transformation — 70
56. Meet the Formula: Single-Sample *z* Tests and *t* Tests — 71
57. Meet the Formula: Comparing Independent Samples and
    Related Samples *t* Tests — 72
58. Meet the Formula: One-Factor Between-Subjects ANOVA — 73
59. Meet the Formula: Two-Factor ANOVA — 76
60. Meet the Formula: One-Factor Within-Subjects ANOVA — 80
61. Meet the Formula: Correlation — 81
62. Meet the Formula: Bivariate Regression — 83

Section 3. Data Analysis Projects — 85
63. Data Analysis Exercise: von Hippel, Ronay, Baker,
    Kjelsaas, and Murphy (2016) — 86
64. Data Analysis Exercise: Nairne, Pandeirada, and Thompson (2008) — 87
65. Data Analysis Project 1: Crammed Versus Distributed Study — 88
66. Data Analysis Project 2: Teaching Techniques Study — 89
67. Data Analysis Project 3: Distracted Driving Study — 90
68. Data Analysis Project 4: Temperature and Air Quality Study — 91
69. Data Analysis Project 5: Job Type and Satisfaction Study — 92
70. Data Analysis Project 6: Attractive Face Recognition Study — 93
71. Data Analysis Project 7: Discrimination in the Workplace Study — 94

Section 4. How to Choose a Statistical Test — 95
72. Using the Flowchart to Find the Correct Statistical Test — 96
73. More Using the Flowchart to Find the Correct Statistical Test — 97
74. Research Design Exercise — 98
75. Design and Data Collection Exercise — 99
76. Designs and Analyses — 101

Section 5. Describing and Interpreting Results in APA Style   **103**

    77. Writing a Results Section From SPSS Output: *t* Tests   104

    78. Writing a Results Section From SPSS Output: ANOVA   105

    79. Interpreting Results Exercise: Sproesser, Schupp, and Renner (2014)   107

    80. Interpreting Results Exercise: Ravizza, Uitvlugt, and Fenn (2017)   108

Appendix: Summary of Formulae   **109**

References   **113**

Preface

This lab manual is meant to accompany a text covering the basic statistics used in the behavioral sciences. It will focus on practicing the statistical skills and concepts you are covering in the course rather than providing the instruction on skills and concepts. In addition, the basics of research design are covered in some activities either on their own or where applicable to accompany statistical analysis.

There are five main sections. The first section contains activities that correspond to topics typically covered in statistics courses. The second section includes activities that examine the underlying statistical formulae with an emphasis on the conceptual similarities and differences among related statistical tests. The third section contains activities related to data analysis projects (including data sets) that students can analyze for analysis projects. The fourth section includes activities designed to help students choose the correct test for different types of data. The fifth section contains exercises designed to help students write up and interpret results from analyses in APA style.

Introduction for Students

Statistical methods are critical tools used in almost all scientific research. As such, gaining a basic understanding of statistical methods and reasoning is essential to both conducting and understanding research findings. However, a good understanding of basic statistical procedures isn't restricted to scientists. You may not realize it, but a good understanding of basic statistics is also extremely useful in one's everyday life as well. As an exercise, go online for a newspaper (or pick one up) or watch the local or national news on television. You'll find many statistical reports; you will be better at recognizing and evaluating them after this course.

Statistics are procedures that are used to summarize sets of data; data are numbers within a context. For example, consider the number 7. By itself, it is an abstraction. However, when considered within a context, it takes on specific meaning. It could represent the number of days that you study for an exam, the score on an exam, the number of questions missed on an exam, or your rank order placement on the exam. It is the context associated with the number that gives the number an interpretable meaning. So, while this course involves abstract manipulation of numbers, it is also concerned with the context associated with the numbers.

This lab manual is meant to accompany a text covering basic statistics used in the behavioral sciences. It will focus on practicing the statistical skills and concepts you are covering in the course, rather than providing the instruction on skills and concepts. Thus, it contains exercises that could be used as homework or lab activities, depending on the structure of your course. We hope that you find these exercises helpful as you practice the statistical skills you are learning.

SECTION 1

Topic Activities

This section of the lab manual includes activities that are designed to help students work through the concepts, calculations, and computer analyses (SPSS® and Excel®) for major topics covered in an introductory statistics course (or in a blended course with research methods). Activities in Section I of the lab manual will also help students work through Excel and SPSS calculations of these statistics and calculations of these statistics by hand, including how to interpret the statistics generated.

Note: SPSS is a registered trademark of International Business Machines Corporation. Excel is a registered trademark of Microsoft Corporation.

1. Statistics in the Media

More than ever before, we are presented with data and statistics in the news. However, most of the time, these analyses are reports of reports (secondary sources). In other words, they are interpreted, summarized, and often simplified by reporters. This exercise is intended to demonstrate the importance of interpreting reports as a critically informed consumer.

Part I

Find an article in the newspaper (online papers are fine) that reports the results of a research finding. (Hint: Check the science section.)

For your chosen article, try to identify as many scientific method details about the research as you can by answering the questions below.

(1) What were the title and authors of the original study upon which the statements in the article are based? What was the hypothesis for the research?

(2) What methodology was used (e.g., experimental, correlational, case study)? Who were the participants and how were they recruited?

(3) What were the conclusions of the research?

(4) What were the limitations of the study? How convinced are you by the study's results?

(5) What questions about the research do you have? What other details were left out that would be useful in evaluating the quality of the study?

Part II

Now try to find the original research article on which the news story was based. You may be able to find the article through a search of Google Scholar or you may need to use a research articles database (e.g., PsycINFO) to search for the original research article. Read the original article, paying close attention to the scientific method details that you summarized earlier and then answer the questions below.

(1) How well do you think the news story conveys the research findings presented in the article? (Hint: Read the abstract summary of the article to get a simple summary of the findings of the study.) Were the original findings accurately portrayed in the news story? Why or why not?

(2) How do you think the popular press article should be changed to provide a more accurate depiction of the original research article published by the researchers?

2. The Purpose of Statistics

Statistics are tools that we use to understand sets of data. Consider the following fictional data set.

A	60	95		H	65	195
B	78	260		I	64	135
C	62	120		J	71	180
D	72	155		K	70	188
E	71	170		L	70	160
F	70	162		M	76	220
G	64	135		N	74	235

Assume that the data set above are the heights (in inches) and weights (in pounds) of 14 students in a class and answer the questions below as best you can.

(1) What does a typical student in this class look like in terms of height and weight?

(2) Is there anyone in the class that has the same height or weight as another student? Identify any students with the same score on the two measures.

(3) What are the highest and lowest weights and heights in the class? What do these values tell you about the group of students in the class?

(4) How do the two different set measures (known as *distributions*) differ? Do you notice anything about these two distributions that distinguishes them?

3. Understanding Your Data

The table below contains a data set that describes the top 25 salaries for major league baseball players as of opening day of the 2016 season:

Player	Team	Position	Age (as of April 28, 2016)	Salary
Kershaw	Dodgers	Pitcher	28	34.57
Greinke	Diamond Backs	Pitcher	32	34
Price	Red Sox	Pitcher	30	30
Verlander	Tigers	Pitcher	33	28
Cabrera	Tigers	1st Base	33	28
Hernandez	Mariners	Pitcher	30	25.85
Sabathia	Yankees	Pitcher	35	25
Lester	Cubs	Pitcher	32	25
Howard	Phillies	1st base	36	25
Pujols	Angels	Designated Hitter	36	25
Cano	Mariners	2nd Base	33	24
Hamels	Rangers	Pitcher	32	23.5
Teixeira	Yankees	1st Base	36	23.13
Mauer	Twins	1st Base	33	23
Ramirez	Red Sox	1st Base	32	22.75
Scherzer	Nationals	Pitcher	31	22.14
Upton	Tigers	Left Field	28	22.13
Tanaka	Yankees	Pitcher	27	22
Reyes	Rockies	Shortstop	32	22
Gonzalez	Dodgers	1st Base	33	21.86
Crawford	Dodgers	Left Field	34	21.61
Werth	Nationals	Left Field	36	21.57
Ellsbury	Yankees	Center Field	32	21.14
Davis	Orioles	1st Base	30	21.12
Shields	Padres	Pitcher	34	21

(1) What are the individuals (i.e., items of analysis) in this data set? Consider what each row in the table above represents to answer this question.

(2) In addition to the players' names, how many variables does the data set contain? Which of these variables take numerical values?

(3) What are the units in which each of the numerical values is expressed? For example, what does it mean when Howard's salary is listed as 25?

(4) What is the most common position in the data set? What is the most common salary? Do you think the most common salary will be the same as the average salary? Why or why not?

4. Research Concepts: Designs, Validity, and Scales of Measurement

1. Does regular exercise reduce the risk of a heart attack? Here are two ways to answer this question:

    Study 1: A researcher finds 2,000 men over age 40 who exercise regularly and have not had heart attacks. She matches each with a similar man who does not exercise regularly, and she follows both groups for five years.

    Study 2: Another researcher finds 4,000 men over age 40 who have not had heart attacks and are willing to participate in a study. He assigns 2,000 of the men to a regular program of supervised exercise. The other 2,000 continue their usual habits. The researcher follows both groups for five years.

    (a) Explain why the first is an observational (i.e., not an experimental) study and the second is an experiment.

    (b) Why does the experiment give more useful information about whether exercise reduces the risk of heart attacks?

2. A researcher evaluates a new growth hormone. One sample of rats is raised with the hormone in their diet and a second sample is raised without the hormone. After six months, the researcher weighs each rat to determine whether the rats in one group are significantly larger than the rats in the other group.

    A second researcher measures femininity for each individual in a group of 10-year-old girls who are all daughters of mothers who work outside of the home. These scores are then compared with corresponding measurements obtained from girls who are all daughters of mothers who work at home. The researcher hopes to show that one group is significantly more feminine than the other.

    What issues with internal and external validity do you think might apply to these studies?

3. Identify the scale of measurement (nominal, ordinal, interval, or ratio) that leads to each of the following conclusions:

    (a) Peter's score is larger than Phil's, but we cannot say how much larger.

    (b) Peter's score is three times larger than Phil's.

    (c) Peter and Phil have different scores, but we cannot say which one is larger, and we cannot determine how much difference there is.

5. Measurement Group Activity

Complete the exercise below and answer the questions within a small group.

(1) Measuring personal characteristics:

- Measure the height of an individual in the group.

  Step 1: Pick one person in your group.

  Step 2: Each person must come up with his or her own way of measuring how tall the volunteer is (including the volunteer himself/herself).

  Step 3: Compare your measurements and answer these questions: What are the pros and cons of each method? What scale of measurement did each of you use (i.e., nominal, ordinal, interval, or ratio)? Which was the most valid measurement (and why)? Which was the most reliable measurement (and why)?

- Measure hair color of individuals in the group. Discuss what it means to measure hair color and answer the following questions:

  (a) Can you use numbers?

  (b) How else can you do it?

  (c) Look around the entire classroom. How many categories of hair color do you see?

- As a group, discuss what needs to be considered in defining categories of hair color.

(2) Measuring indirectly observable characteristics:

- Suppose that your group is a set of researchers interested in studying factors that impact how extroverted (i.e., outgoing) people are. To investigate extroversion, imagine that you have decided to develop an instrument to measure the "out-goingness" of each student in your class (we won't actually collect any data; just think about how we would do it). Discuss how you would go about developing an instrument to measure this character trait. What observations/measurements would you make? What would your concerns be about validity and reliability be? What scale of measurement would you use?

(3) Scale of Measurement:

For the following measurements, decide what scale of measurement is used (nominal, ordinal, interval, or ratio).

(a) Shoe size is measured with standard adult shoe sizes, such as 7, 8, 8 ½, 9, 9 ½, 10, 11, and so on.

(b) Foot length is measured in centimeters.

(c) You collect data about what type of cell phone each person in the class has.

(d) You determine hand dominance (i.e., which hand people use for most tasks) for the members of your class.

6. Designing an Experiment Group Activity

Complete this exercise in a small group:

Your group's task is to take an issue below (assigned to your group by your instructor or picked by your group) and design an experiment (or series of experiments, if you deem it necessary) to examine it.

    (1)   Does watching violence on TV cause violent behavior?

    (2)   Does playing video games improve hand–eye coordination in other tasks?

    (3)   Does smoking cause lung cancer?

    (4)   Does studying with background music improve test scores?

    (5)   Does living in a large city decrease helping behaviors?

    (6)   Does color affect mood?

    (7)   Does caffeine affect work productivity?

Be sure to include information about what your variables are, how you will manipulate your independent variables, how you will measure your dependent variables, what control conditions you need, who your participants are, and so on. Make sure that you give enough thought and detailed discussion to all of these issues to design a good study to answer the question.

    (1)   Individually, provide a description of the experiment that your group designed (including the information mentioned above).

    (2)   Now spend some time evaluating the experiment that your group designed. You should consider

- the adequacy of the way the dependent variable(s) is/are measured.
- the adequacy of the way the independent variable(s) is/are manipulated.
- if there are enough appropriate control conditions.
- what (if any) threats there are to internal and external validity.
- what potential confounds there are.
- how you would describe the design of your experiment.

9. Displaying Distributions

Create a frequency table including the range of responses, frequency, proportion, percentage, cumulative proportion, and cumulative frequency for the following data illustrating the number of correct responses on a quiz:

1, 4, 3, 2, 3, 4, 5, 2, 3, 5, 5, 3, 2, 1, 4, 3, 2, 3, 1, 3, 4, 3, 2, 4

(1) What percentage of students scored a 3 or lower on the quiz?

(2) Create a frequency distribution graph of the data. What is the shape of this distribution?

(3) What is a typical score in the distribution? What do you know about this score in the distribution?

10. Setting Up Your Data in SPSS: Creating a Data File

Create a data file in SPSS based on the data below and then answer the questions below.

ID#568 Name: Joe Hart Age: 25 Gender: Male Income: $23,000 IQ: 105	ID#: 276 Name: Mary Swanson Age: 37 Gender: Female Income: $41,000 IQ: 115	ID#: 384 Name: Sam Lewis Age: 61 Gender: Male Income: $56,000 IQ: 125
ID#: 866 Name: Chin Lee Age: 32 Gender: Male Income: $36,000 IQ: 140	ID#: 231 Name: Al Walton Age: 39 Gender: Male Income: $29,000 IQ: 95	ID#: 476 Sara Smith Age: 27 Gender: Female Income: $18,000 IQ: 90
ID#: 007 Name: David Dodge Age: 34 Gender: Male Income: $29,000 IQ: 115	ID#: 627 Name: Michelle Friedlander Age: 38 Gender: Female Income: $22,000 IQ: 105	

(1) How many individuals are in your data set? Does this match the number of rows in your SPSS data window?

(2) How many variables are in your data set? Does this match the number of columns in your SPSS data window?

(3) Which of your variables are categorical variables? Which are continuous variables?

(4) For each variable, what measure of central tendency would you report?

11. Displaying Distributions in SPSS

Part I

Use the Student_1.sav data file (http://psychology.illinoisstate.edu/jccutti/StatsDataFiles/students_1.sav) to create a frequency distribution table for the Quiz 1 variable using SPSS. Then answer the questions below using your table.

(1)   What percentage of the scores is at or below a score of 7?

(2)   Where does it appear that most of the scores are located?

(3)   What does your answer tell you about the difficulty of the quiz?

Part II

Now create a frequency distribution table using SPSS for the Quiz 2 variable. Compare this table to the one you created in Part I to answer the questions below.

(4)   For which quiz do the scores appear to be more evenly distributed across the scale?

(5)   Which quiz appeared to be harder? How do you know this?

12. Basic Probability

Consider the following populations and samples. For each, try to decide which population the sample was more likely to have been drawn from.

(1) A standard deck (we'll call it Population 1) has 52 cards: one card for numbers 2 through 10 and a Jack, Queen, King, and Ace for each of the four suits (♥, ♦, ♣, ♠).

A Pinochle deck (we'll call it Population 2) has 48 cards: one card for numbers 2 through 8 and two for 9 through Ace (9, 10, Jack, Queen, King, Ace) for each of the four suits (♥, ♦, ♣, ♠).

If you were dealt 9♥, 10♠, J♣, K♠, A♥ (our sample), which deck (population) is this hand more likely to have come from? Explain your answer. How certain do you feel about your choice?

(2) At the local game store, you pick up two 6-sided dice. One die is a true die: the chances of rolling a 1, 2, 3, 4, 5, or 6 are all equivalent. The other die is a loaded die that has been weighted so that the 1 happens very infrequently, the 6 occurs more frequently than usual, and the 2, 3, 4, and 5 occur at their normal rates. The two dice look the same and you forget which is which. You decide to pick one of them and roll it 6 times (our sample). Suppose that your sample roll is 1, 1, 3, 2, 6, 2. Which die do you think you selected, the true die or the loaded die? Explain your answer. How certain do you feel about your choice?

13. Sampling

1. Your college wants to gather student opinion about parking for students on campus. It isn't practical to contact all students.

   (a) Design a bad sample. Give an example of a way to choose a sample of students that is poor practice because it depends on voluntary response.

   (b) Design another bad sample. Give an example of a way to choose a sample of students that is poor practice that doesn't involve voluntary response.

   (c) Design a good sample. Give an example of a way to choose a sample of students that is good practice.

2. Suppose that a University Club has 25 student (S) members and 10 faculty (F) members. Their names are as follows:

Barrett	S	Duncan	S	Hu	S	Lee	S	Reeder	F
Bergner	F	Frazier	S	Jarvis	F	Main	S	Ren	S
Brady	S	Gibellato	S	Jimenez	S	McBride	F	Santos	S
Chen	S	Gulati	S	Kahn	F	Nemeth	S	Sroka	S
Critchfield	F	Han	S	Katsaounis	S	O'Rourke	S	Tobin	F
Desouza	F	Hostetler	S	Kim	S	Paul	S	Tordoff	S
Draper	S	House	F	Kohlschmidt	S	Pryor	F	Wang	S

Assuming that the club may send only one person to an international conference,

   (a) what are the odds of sending Dr. Tobin to the conference?

   (b) what are the odds of sending a student to the conference?

   (c) what are the odds of sending somebody with the last name that begins with the letter K?

14. Central Tendency 1

For each data set below, calculate the mean, median, and mode. Then answer the questions that follow.

(1) Data set 1: 21, 22, 23, 24, 24, 24, 25, 25, 25, 25, 26, 27, 28

    (a) Mean:

    (b) Median:

    (c) Mode:

(2) Data set 2: 20, 20, 20, 21, 21, 21, 21, 21, 27, 27, 28, 28, 28, 28

    (a) Mean:

    (b) Median:

    (c) Mode:

(3) Which data set has the highest mean?

(4) Is the mean the best measure of central tendency for these two distributions? Why or why not?

15. Central Tendency 2

1. What is the value of the mean, median, and mode for the following set of scores?

    Scores: 1, 3, 5, 0, 1, 3

2. In a sample of $n = 6$, five individuals all have a score of 10 and the sixth person has a score of 16. What is the mean for this sample?

3. After 5 points are added to every score in a distribution, the mean is calculated and found to be 30. What was the value of the mean for the original distribution?

4. For a perfectly symmetrical distribution with mean = 30, what is the value of the median?

5. For the following set of scores, identify which measure would provide the best description of central tendency and explain your answer.

    Scores: 0, 30, 31, 33, 33, 34, 35, 37, 38

16. Central Tendency in SPSS

For this exercise, use the downloadable Student_1.sav data file (http://psychology.illinoisstate.edu/jccutti/StatsDataFiles/students_1.sav).

(1) Using SPSS for your computations, answer the following questions.

    (a) What is the mean for the final variable?

    (b) What is the median for the final variable?

    (c) What is the mode for the final variable?

    (d) What percentage of students scored lower than the mode on the final? (Hints: Don't include the students who scored the mode exactly. Don't include % in your answer. Round to one digit. Thus, 22.2% would be entered as 22.2.)

(2) Look at the distribution in the histogram below to answer the questions.

    (a) From lowest to highest, list the mean, median, and mode.

    (b) Of the three measures of central tendency (mean, median, and mode), which is the least representative number for this distribution?

    (c) Which type of skew (positive or negative) is evident in this distribution?

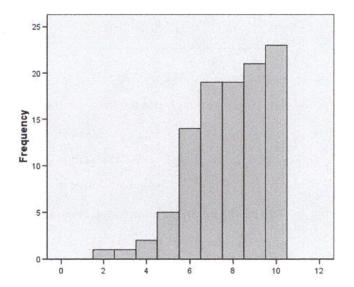

17. Describing a Distribution by Hand

Suppose that you conducted a survey examining how much your friends ($n = 10$) like a "how to study" website and if their rating of the site is related to their grade point average (GPA). Your survey's response scale runs from 0 = *do not like at all* to 5 = *absolutely love*. Your sample of 10 has these results for the survey (X): 5, 1, 2, 4, 3, 2, 4, 3, 0, 3.

1. Display results in a frequency distribution table and a histogram.

Frequency Distribution Table and Histogram

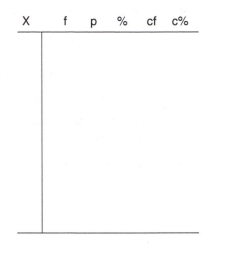
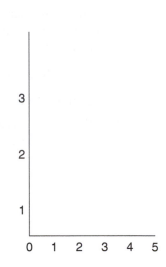

2. Find measures of central tendency for the sample:

$$\text{Mean} =$$

$$\text{Median} =$$

$$\text{Mode} =$$

3. Provide the following information about the sample (where p stands for *probability of*):

$$p(X = 3) =$$

$$p(X > 0) =$$

$$p(0 < X < 4) =$$

$$p(X > 4) =$$

18. More Describing Distributions

1. In a population of $N = 10$ scores, the smallest score is $X = 8$ and the largest score is $X = 20$. The range of the population is _____.

2. In a sample of $n = 5$ scores, the mean is 20 and $s^2 = 4$. What is the sample standard deviation?

3. A population of scores has a mean of 50 and standard deviation of 12. If you subtract five points from every score in the population, then the value of the new standard deviation will be _____.

4. What is the value of the sum of squares (SS) for the following scores?

   Scores: 1, 1, 1, 3

5. Compute the SS, variance, and standard deviation for the following population of scores.

   Scores: 9, 1, 8, 6

19. Descriptive Statistics Exercise

Below are data from a fictional two-factor between-subjects experiment. Compute the mean and standard deviation for each condition according to the instructions given using the tables provided. In addition, compute the marginal means for both factors.

Dr. Readalot conducted a study examining the effectiveness of different kinds of studying. He had students study either for five hours the night before the test (crammed study) or for one hour each of the five nights prior to the test (distributed study). Additionally, he was interested in whether the kind of material being studied (and tested) would interact with the method of studying (math or vocabulary). He tested five participants in each of the four conditions. The test score (in percentage correct) for each participant is presented in the table below.

(1) Compute the condition and independent variable level means and enter them into the table below.

Factor A: Math or Vocabulary Questions Factor B: Crammed or Distributed Practice			Marginal Means for Type of Studying
	Math	Vocabulary	
Crammed	87	90	
	65	84	
	72	72	
	73	78	
	53	76	
	_____	_____	
	M:	M:	
	SD:	SD:	
Distributed	88	98	
	75	89	
	82	79	
	75	84	
	80	100	
	_____	_____	
	M:	M:	
	SD:	SD:	
Marginal Means: for Type of Material			

(2) Now use the table above to compute the crammed math condition standard deviation.

Step 1: Subtract the mean from each score in the condition (these are the deviations).	Step 2: Square each of the deviations.	Step 3: Add up the squared deviations (sum of squared deviations, SS).	Step 4: Divide SS by n–1 (number of scores minus one). This gives you the variance.	Step 5: Take the square root of the variance. This gives you your standard deviation.
87 – ____ = ____	____			
65 – ____ = ____	____	____	____ = ____	√____ = ____
72 – ____ = ____	____		(5–1)	
73 – ____ = ____	____			
53 – ____ = ____	____			

(3) Finally, compute the standard deviations for the other three conditions in the study in the same way, making your own table of steps for each condition.

(4) Enter all your standard deviations into the first table to complete that table.

20. Descriptive Statistics With Excel

One widely available program for calculating descriptive statistics is Microsoft Excel. Excel is a spreadsheet program that can be used by researchers to manage and analyze data sets. The following exercise is designed to introduce you to some of the basic descriptive statistical resources within Excel that may be useful in your course.

Use the data listed below and Excel to compute the means and standard deviations for each condition.

	A	B
	Control	Treatment
1	45	64
2	65	76
3	75	83
4	56	69
5	46	66

21. Measures of Variability in SPSS

1. Open Student_1.sav data file (http://psychology.illinoisstate.edu/jccutti/StatsDataFiles/students_1.sav). Use this file and SPSS to answer these questions:

    (a) What are the mean, standard deviation, and range for Quizzes 1–5?

    (b) Which quiz has the largest variability based on range? Based on standard deviation?

2. Consider the following three distributions of data:

Distribution 1	Distribution 2	Distribution 3
1, 2, 3, 3, 4, 4, 4, 5, 5, 5, 5, 5, 6, 6, 6, 7, 7, 8, 9, 9	3, 3, 3, 3, 4, 4, 4, 5, 5, 5, 5, 5, 6, 6, 6, 7, 7, 7, 7, 8	1, 3, 3, 4, 4, 5, 5, 5, 5, 5, 5, 5, 5, 5, 6, 6, 6, 7, 7, 9

    Type the data from the three distributions into a new file in SPSS.

    (a) By only looking at the numbers, for which distribution is variability the lowest? Why did you come to that conclusion?

    (b) For each distribution, use SPSS to construct a histogram and compute the range and standard deviation.

    (c) Which measure of variability is most affected by extreme values? (Hint: Compare the second and third distributions.)

22. Calculating *z* Scores Using SPSS

1. Open the data file CSdata.sav (http://psychology.illinoisstate.edu/jccutti/StatsDataFiles/ CSdata.sav) in SPSS. Plot a histogram of math SAT scores of the students in this file (satm).

2. Convert every score in the distribution (math SAT) to a *z* score with SPSS.

    (a) Using SPSS, make a histogram of the new *zsatm* variable. What does it look like (what is the shape)? How does it compare to the original *satm* histogram?

    (b) What is the mean and standard deviation? Explain why we get these values for the mean and standard deviation. (Think about the *z* score formula.)

Using Standard Scores to Compare Different Distributions

Consider the following two standardized distributions:

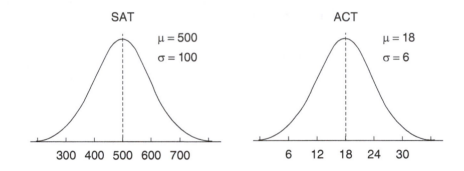

3. Suppose that you got a 540 on the SAT and a 20 on the ACT for the distributions described above. Which score is better?

4. Suppose that you got a 600 on the SAT and a 24 on the ACT. Which score is better?

23. The Normal Distribution

1. Answer the following questions about the normal distribution:

   (a) What percentage of the area under the curve is between the mean and the right-most end of the curve?

   (b) What percentage of the area under the curve is within one standard deviation of the mean (on either side of the mean)?

2. Using the Unit Normal Table, determine the following:

   (a) Find the probabilities that correspond to the following z scores: 2.0, 0.5, –0.75, –2.0

   (b) Find the z scores that correspond to the following probabilities: 0.5000, 0.8413, 0.3050

3. Assume that the following is true: The scale for the SAT is set so that the distribution of scores is approximately normal with mean = 500 and standard deviation = 100.

   (a) What is the probability of having an SAT score of 130 or above?

   (b) What is the probability of having an SAT score of 120 or above?

   (c) What is the probability of having an SAT score of 91 or less?

   (d) You think that you might need a tutor. You know of a tutoring service for students who score between 350 and 650 on the SAT. You think that you probably fit within their range. What is the probability that you will get an SAT score between 350 and 650?

   (e) The National Collegiate Athletic Association (NCAA) requires Division I athletes to score at least 820 on the combined mathematics and verbal parts of the SAT exam in order to compete in their first college year. In 1999, the scores of the millions of students taking the SATs were approximately normal with a mean = 1017 and a standard deviation = 209. What is the probability of scoring an 820 or less in this distribution?

24. *z* Scores and the Normal Distribution

Use the following means and standard deviations: for ACT, $\mu = 21$, $\sigma = 3$ and for SAT, $\mu = 500$, $\sigma = 100$.

(1) You take the ACT test and the SAT test. You get a 24 on the ACT and a 660 on the SAT. The college that you apply to only needs one score. Which do you want to send them (that is, which score is better: 24 or 660?). Why?

(2) What is the probability of having an ACT score of 20 or less?

(3) What SAT score do you need to have to be in the top 15% of the population?

(4) What is the probability of scoring between 500 and 650 on the SAT?

(5) What is your percentile rank if you have an ACT of 25.5?

25. Hypothesis Testing With Normal Populations

1. Each of the following situations calls for a significance test of a population mean. State the null hypothesis H_0 and the alternative hypothesis H_a in each case.

   (a) The diameter of a spindle in a small motor is supposed to be 5mm. If the spindle is either too small or too large, the motor will not work properly. The manufacturer measures the diameter in a sample of motors to determine whether the mean diameter has moved away from the target.

   (b) Census Bureau data show that the mean household income in the area served by a shopping mall is $52,500 per year. A market research firm questions shoppers at the mall. The researchers suspect the mean household income of mall shoppers is higher than that of the general population.

   (c) The examinations in a large psychology class are scaled after grading so that the mean score is 50. The professor thinks that one teaching assistant is a poor teacher and suspects that his students have a lower mean than the class as a whole. The teaching assistant's students this semester can be considered a sample from the population of all students in the course, so the professor compares their mean score with 50.

2. A researcher would like to test the effectiveness of a newly developed growth hormone. The researcher knows that under normal circumstances, laboratory rats reach an average weight of 1,000 grams at 10 weeks of age. When the sample of 10 rats is weighed at 10 weeks, they weigh 1,010 grams.

   (a) Assuming that the growth hormone has no effect, what would a Type I error be in this situation?

   (b) Assuming that the growth hormone does have an effect, what would a Type II error be in this situation?

26. Stating Hypotheses and Choosing Tests

For each of the following scenarios, identify

    (a)   whether a one-tailed test can be used or if a two-tailed test is more appropriate (remember to use a one-tailed whenever you can find a directional alternative hypothesis to increase power).

    (b)   the null and alternative hypotheses.

    (c)   the appropriate statistical test.

        (1)   People with agoraphobia are so filled with anxiety about being in public places that they seldom leave their homes. Knowing this is a difficult disorder to treat, a researcher tries a long-term treatment. A sample of individuals reports how often they have ventured out of the house in the past month. Then they receive relaxation training and are introduced to trips away from the house at gradually increasing durations. After two months of treatment, subjects report the number of trips out of the house they made in the last 30 days. The researcher wants to determine if the number of trips out of the house has increased after the treatment.

        (2)   An experiment studied the effect of diet on blood pressure. Researchers randomly divided 54 healthy adults into two groups. One group received a calcium supplement. The other received a placebo. Blood pressure was measured at the end of one month.

        (3)   Suppose that during interpersonal social interactions (e.g., during business meetings or talking to casual acquaintances), people in the United States maintain an average distance of $\mu = 7$ feet from other people. The distribution of distance scores is normal with a $\sigma = 1.5$ feet. A researcher examines how people in the United States compare in social interaction distance to social interaction distance for people in Italy. A random sample of 40 Italians is observed during interpersonal interactions. For this sample, the mean interaction distance is 4.5 feet. Do the Italians have closer social interactions than Americans do?

        (4)   The animal learning course in a university's psychology department requires that each student train a rat to perform certain behaviors. The student's grade is partially determined by the rat's performance. The instructor for the course has noticed that some students are very comfortable working with the rats and seem to be very successful training their rats. The instructor suspects that that these students may have previous experience with pets that gives them an advantage in the class. To test this hypothesis, the instructor gives the entire class a questionnaire at the beginning of the course. One question determines if each student currently has a pet of any type at home. Based on the responses to this question, the instructor divides the class into two groups and compares the rats' learning scores for the two groups.

        (5)   A scientist investigated the authenticity of extrasensory perception (ESP) by asking subjects who claimed to have ESP to predict the symbol that would appear on the back side of a succession of cards. Each card had a square, a circle, a star, or a triangle. Subjects were informed of this fact and were asked to predict what was on the back of each card as it was held up to them. Because the subjects could not see the backs of the cards, if they had no ESP and simply guessed, they would get an average of 0.25 answers correct ($\mu = 0.25$). The scientist measured how many answers the subjects got correct out of 100 cards.

(6) A researcher is interested in how the values taught to students by their parents influence their academic achievement. The parents of one group of students is asked to follow a program in which they spend one hour per day discussing homework assignments with their child. In the other group, parents are given no program to follow. To control for genetic influences on academic achievement, the subjects in the study are identical twins raised apart (i.e., by different parents). One of the twins is randomly assigned to one group and the other twin is placed in the other group. Academic achievement is measured by grade point average at the end of the first year of high school.

27. Hypothesis Testing With z Tests

1. Suppose we think that listening to classical music will affect the amount of time it takes a person to fall asleep; we conduct a study to test this idea.

    (a) Suppose that the average person in the population falls asleep in 15 minutes (without listening to classical music) with $\sigma = 6$ minutes. State the null and alternative hypotheses for this study.

    (b) Assume that the amount of time it takes people in the population to fall asleep is normally distributed. In the study, we have a sample of people listen to classical music and then we measure how long it takes them to fall asleep. Suppose the sample of 36 people fall asleep in 12 minutes. What is the probability of obtaining a sample mean of 12 minutes or smaller? Assuming $\alpha = 0.05$, is your calculated p value in the critical region? (Hint: Remember to consider two critical regions.)

    (c) Using your answer above, what decision should be made about your null hypothesis?

    (d) Assume now that in reality, classical music does not affect how long it takes people to fall asleep. In this case, what kind of decision (correct, Type I error, or Type II error) have you made in (c)?

2. A psychologist examined the effect of chronic alcohol abuse on memory. In this study, a standardized memory test was used. Scores on this test for the general population form a normal distribution with $\mu = 50$ and $\sigma = 6$. A sample of $n = 22$ alcohol abusers had a mean score of $\overline{X} = 47$. Is there evidence for memory impairment among alcoholics? Use $\alpha = 0.05$ for a one-tailed test. Write out each step of hypothesis testing.

3. On a vocational interest inventory that measures interest in several categories, a very large standardization group of adults (i.e., a population) has an average score of $\mu = 22$ and $\sigma = 4$. Scores are normally distributed. A researcher would like to determine if scientists differ from the general population in terms of writing interests. A random sample of scientists is selected from the directory of a national science society. The scientists are given the inventory, and their test scores on the literary scale are as follows: 21, 20, 23, 28, 30, 24, 23, 19. Do scientists differ from the general population in their writing interests? Test at the 0.05 level of significance for two tails. Write out each step of hypothesis testing.

28. Hypothesis Testing With a Single Sample

Consider the following scenarios. For each one, determine which formula (z or t) is appropriate to use to answer the question asked. (You don't need to do any computations.)

(1) Pat, a personal trainer would like to examine the effects of humidity on exercise behavior. It is known that the average person in the United States exercises an average of $\mu = 21$ minutes each day. The personal trainer selects a random sample of $n = 100$ people and places them in a controlled atmosphere environment where the relative humidity is maintained at 90%. The daily amount of time spent exercising for the sample averages 18.7 minutes with $s = 5.0$.

(2) In an attempt to regulate the profession, the U.S. Department of Fitness has developed a fitness test for personal trainers. The test requires that the trainers must perform a series of exercises within a certain period of time. Normative data, collected in a nationwide test, reveal a normal distribution with an average completion time of $\mu = 92$ minutes and of $\sigma = 11$. Pat and four other Hollywood personal trainers ($n = 5$) take the test. For these trainers, the average time to complete the task averages 115 minutes. Pat is worried that the Hollywood personal trainers in this sample differ significantly from the norm.

(3) Now let's conduct the hypothesis tests for the examples above. Complete the hypothesis test for the tests you choose for (1) and (2) above (z or t test), showing all the steps.

29. One-Sample *t* Test in SPSS

Use SPSS to complete the one-sample *t* test and answer the questions for each study example below.

(1) Suppose that your psychology professor, Dr. I. D. Ego, gives a 20-point true/false quiz to nine students and wants to know if they are different from groups in the past, who have tended to have an average of 9. Their scores from the current group are 6, 7, 7, 8, 8, 8, 9, 9, 10. Did the current group perform differently from those in the past? Assume a critical value of $\alpha = 0.05$.

(2) The personnel department for a major corporation in the Northeast reported that the average number of absences during the months of January and February last year was $\mu = 7.4$. In an attempt to reduce absences, the company offered free flu shots to all employees this year. For a sample of $n = 10$ people who took the flu shots, the number of absences this year were 6, 8, 10, 3, 4, 6, 5, 4, 5, 6. Do these data indicate a significant reduction in the number of absences? Use $\alpha = 0.05$.

30. One-Sample *t* Tests by Hand

Use a one-sample *t* test (calculated by hand) to answer the questions below:

(1) Suppose that your psychology professor, Dr. I. D. Ego, wants to evaluate people's driving ability after 24 hours of sleep deprivation. She develops a test of driving skill (scores ranging from 1 = bad driving to 10 = excellent driving) and administers it to 101 drivers who have been paid to stay awake for 24 hrs. The scores from the group had a mean of 4.5 and a standard deviation of 1.6. Determine if the sleep-deprived group mean is significantly different from the known population mean of 5.8 for the driving test. Assume $\alpha = 0.05$.

(2) Several years ago, a school survey revealed that the average age at which students first tried an alcoholic beverage was $\mu = 14$ years (with a normal distribution). To determine if anything has changed, a random sample of five students was asked questions about alcohol use. The age at which drinking first began was reported as 11, 13, 14, 12, 10. Use these data to determine if there has been a change in the age at which drinking began. Use $\alpha = 0.05$.

(3) A random sample of $n = 36$ scores has $\overline{X} = 48$. Use this sample ($\alpha = 0.05$) to determine if the sample is different from the population with $\mu = 45$ for each of the following situations:

(a) Sample $SS = 60$

(b) Sample $SS = 600$

How does the sample variability contribute to the outcome of the test?

(4) A national company is attempting to determine if they need to hire more employees. One thing they are basing this decision on is the number of hours per week their current employees work. They collect a sample of average hours worked per week from 30 employees to compare with the national full-time work standard of 40 hours per week. The mean number of hours worked for their sample is 47.8 with $SS = 1020$. Using $\alpha = 0.05$, conduct a test to determine if this company's employees work more hours per week than the national standard.

(5) Scores on the SAT test are normally distributed with $\mu = 500$ and $\sigma = 100$. Dr. Ed Standards, the local district school superintendent, develops a new program that he believes should increase SAT scores for students. He selects 25 local high school students to participate in the program and then take the SAT test. His sample has an average SAT score of 559. Conduct a hypothesis test to determine if this program works. Show all your steps and state all your assumptions.

(6) Suppose that the school board tells Dr. Standards that the new program is too expensive to pilot on 25 students and asks that he reduce his sample size to 9 students. Assume the same properties for the population of SAT scores. Suppose that his sample of 9 students also has a mean score of 559. How does this reduction in sample size affect Dr. Standards's hypothesis test?

31. Related Samples *t* Tests

1. A major university would like to improve its tarnished image following a large on-campus scandal. Its marketing department develops a short television commercial and tests it on a sample of $n = 7$ subjects. People's attitudes about the university are measured with a short questionnaire both before and after viewing the commercial. The data are as follows:

Person	X_1 (Before)	X_2 (After)
A	15	15
B	11	13
C	10	18
D	11	12
E	14	16
F	10	10
G	11	19
H	10	20
I	12	13
J	15	18

(a) Is this a within-subjects or a matched samples design? Explain your answer.

(b) Conduct a hypothesis test (showing all the steps) to determine if the university should spend money to air the commercial (i.e., did the commercial improve the attitudes?) Assume an alpha level = 0.05.

2. For the sample difference scores below, determine if the sample differs from $D = 0$. Use $\alpha = 0.01$.

Difference scores (D): 4, 5, 4, 2, 4, 5, 3, 5, 4

3. A researcher was interested in environmental effects on handedness. He measured the handedness of twins raised apart, where a positive score indicates more right-handedness and a negative score indicates more left-handedness (a score of zero means the subject is ambidextrous). He used matched pairs of identical twins as subjects to rule out any genetic contribution to handedness scores (identical twins are the same genetically). The scores for each pair of twins are listed below. Use these data to determine if the twins differ in handedness score (indicating that environment plays a role in handedness). Use $\alpha = 0.05$.

Pair	Handedness Score Twin A	Twin B
1	+10	+11
2	−8	+3
3	−11	+11
4	+15	+10
5	0	+8
6	−4	+7

4. Each of the following sets of sample statistics comes from a within-subjects design.

$$\text{Set 1: } n = 10, \overline{D} = +4.0, s = 10$$

$$\text{Set 2: } n = 10, \overline{D} = +4.0, s = 2$$

Find t values. Without looking up the critical t, for which set is it more likely to reject the H_0 indicating that the $\mu_D = 0$? Why?

32. Related Samples t Test in SPSS

1. A psychology instructor teaches statistics. She wants to know if her lectures are helping her students understand the material. She tells students to read the chapter in the textbook before coming to class. Then, before lecturing, the professor gives her class ($n = 10$) a short quiz on the material. Then she lectures on the same topic and follows her lecture with another quiz on the same material. Is there an effect by her lecture? Assume $\alpha = 0.05$. The data are as follows:

Person	X_1 (Before)	X_2 (After)
A	85	85
B	81	83
C	70	78
D	91	92
E	84	88
F	70	70
G	91	89
H	80	90
I	72	73
J	85	88

(a) Enter the data into SPSS. Test your H_0 using a paired samples t test. Do you reject the H_0?

(b) Use the Compute function to make a new variable that is the difference between the after-lecture quiz and the before-lecture quiz. Now use SPSS to compute a one-sample t test on this new difference column (use zero as your test value). How do the results of this test compare with your earlier answer? Why do you think this occurred?

33. Independent Samples *t* Tests

1. A psychologist is interested in studying the effects of fatigue on mental alertness. She decides to study this question using a between-subjects design. She randomly assigns individuals to two groups (Group 1 stays awake for 24 hours; Group 2 goes to sleep). After this period, each subject is tested to see how well they detect a light on a screen. The dependent variable is the subjects' number of mistakes, which reflects their mental alertness. The higher the number, the less alert they are. Here are the results from the two groups.

	Group 1 (Awake)	Group 2 (Sleep)
n	5	10
mean	35	24
SS	120	270

Using an independent samples *t* test, answer the question of whether fatigue adversely affects mental alertness ($\alpha = 0.05$). (Do this test by hand.)

2. A psychology instructor at a large university teaches statistics. There are 22 students in the class, and he has broken them into two groups. Each group has a different graduate assistant who is responsible for running separate breakout lecture and lab sections of the course. One graduate assistant (GA) has lots of experience teaching while the other has more limited experience. The instructor wants to check for comparable learning across the two GAs, hoping to find no difference. The data below are the scores (out of 100) of the students on the first midterm. Is there a difference between the groups? Assume $\alpha = 0.05$. The data are as follows (notice that one group has more students than the other):

Group 1 (Less-Experienced GA)	Group 2 (More-Experienced GA)
60	70
65	85
69	72
58	83
57	81
59	69
52	65
72	75
70	79
65	71
	89
	80

34. Hypothesis Testing: Multiple Tests

1. A between-subjects design was conducted to compare two groups. Data included the following:

    $$\overline{X}_A = 58, \overline{X}_B = 52$$

    $$n_A = 4, n_B = 4$$

    $$SS_A = 84, SS_B = 108$$

    (a) Calculate the variance for each sample and then compute the pooled variance. You should find that the pooled variance is exactly halfway between the two sample variances. Why is this true for this particular study?

    (b) Do these data indicate a significant difference between the groups? Use a two-tailed test with $\alpha = 0.05$.

2. For two samples, one sample has $n = 6$ and $SS = 500$, while the other sample has $n = 9$ and $SS = 670$. If the sample mean difference is 15 points, is this difference large enough to be significant for $\alpha = 0.05$ with a two-tailed test?

3. Two people are arguing about the size of different breeds of dogs. One believes that German shepherds are larger than huskies, while the other person believes the opposite is true. They conduct a study to see which one of them is correct. They sample the weights of 10 dogs of each breed. The data are as follows:

    German Shepherds: 55, 72, 61, 43, 59, 70, 67, 49, 55, 63

    Huskies: 48, 77, 46, 51, 60, 44, 53, 61, 52, 41

    (a) Should a one-tailed or two-tailed test be conducted? Why?

    (b) Conduct the appropriate test with $\alpha = 0.05$. Which breed is larger or are they the same?

4. Different designs affect the following set of data. Both tests will try to find any difference between treatments with $\alpha = 0.05$. (These data can represent either 10 different participants or five participants tested in each condition.)

Treatment 1	Treatment 2
10	11
2	5
1	2
15	18
7	9

    (a) Assume that the data are from an independent samples experiment using two separate samples, each with five subjects. Use SPSS to test whether the data indicate a significant difference between the two treatments (assume $\alpha = 0.05$). List each step of the hypothesis-testing procedure.

(b) Now assume that the data are from a repeated-measures design using one sample of five subjects, each of whom have been tested twice. Use SPSS to test whether the data indicate a significant difference between the two treatments (again, assume $\alpha = 0.05$). Remember that you'll have to change the way the data are entered in the data window.

(c) You should find that the repeated-measures design and the independent samples design reach a different conclusion. How do you explain the differences? (Hint: Think about how sampling error is estimated for the two tests.)

35. More Hypothesis Tests With Multiple Tests

1. A marine biologist is comparing the size of great white sharks in the Pacific and Atlantic Oceans to determine which ocean has the larger sharks. He takes a sample of 20 sharks (10 sharks from each ocean) and measures their lengths. The measurements for the 20 sharks are listed below:

Shark Length (in Feet)			
Pacific Ocean		Atlantic Ocean	
1	18.2	11	16.1
2	15.8	12	14.3
3	13.6	13	14.7
4	19.7	14	15.7
5	19.1	15	19.6
6	12.2	16	15.3
7	16.8	17	13.2
8	22.8	18	15.8
9	16.6	19	15.2
10	16.8	20	16.2

2. A behavioral psychologist wants to know if food acts as a good motivator for rats to learn a maze faster than normal. She places a food pellet at the end of a maze that the rat can smell while working through the maze. She puts eight rats through the maze and records how long it takes them to find the food at the end. She already knows that without the food, rats as a population take an average of 28.9 seconds to run the maze (with a normal distribution). Using the timing data recorded below, determine if the rats learn the maze faster with the food pellet than without it.

    Times in seconds ($n = 8$): 25.6, 29.0, 23.1, 25.5, 28.7, 26.5, 25.4, 23.9

3. Two groups of participants ($n = 10$ per group, total $N = 20$) were given a problem-solving task. One group was told they had five minutes to complete the task. The other group was not told they had a time limit but was also given five minutes to complete the task. For both groups, the number of puzzles solved in the five-minute period was measured. The data for the 20 participants are listed below. Conduct a hypothesis test to determine if an announced time limit affects the number of puzzles solved. Based on the outcome of the test, what can you conclude about the effect of an announced time limit?

Number Solved			
Time Limit Announced		No Time Limit Announced	
S1	6	S11	7
S2	8	S12	6
S3	5	S13	9
S4	4	S14	4
S5	6	S15	8
S6	9	S16	10
S7	8	S17	7
S8	5	S18	8
S9	4	S19	7
S10	5	S20	9

4. Does caffeine reduce depression? Participants in this study were 10 people who regularly consume something containing caffeine each day. During the study, however, each participant was barred from consuming caffeine not provided by the experimenter. They came to the lab two subsequent mornings and were given a pill. The pill either contained caffeine or was a placebo (i.e., each participant received both pills but on different days). The order of the pill received was counterbalanced (i.e., half of the group received the caffeine pill the first day and the other half received it the second). They completed a depression scale at the end of each day. Based on the depression scores below (higher scores mean more depression), does caffeine appear to reduce depression?

Depression Scores		
Person	Caffeine	Placebo
1	5	16
2	5	23
3	4	5
4	3	7
5	8	14
6	5	24
7	0	6
8	0	3
9	2	15
10	11	12

5.   Whether a winning team can be purchased is a debated topic in baseball. Many major league team owners spend a lot of money on talented players to put together a team that they hope will win. Using the data below on 20 teams, conduct a test to compare batting averages for samples of players from the 10 teams with the highest payroll and teams with the 10 teams with the lowest payrolls to see if this practice is justified.

Batting Averages			
Highest Payroll		Lowest Payroll	
Team 1	.275	Team 11	.289
Team 2	.301	Team 12	.255
Team 3	.225	Team 13	.267
Team 4	.325	Team 14	.333
Team 5	.350	Team 15	.233
Team 6	.210	Team 16	.300
Team 7	.240	Team 17	.245
Team 8	.200	Team 18	.285
Team 9	.315	Team 19	.292
Team 10	.301	Team 20	.310

36. *t* Tests Summary Worksheet

A number of studies have tested how the amount of sleep one gets affects test performance. In Study 1, a single sample was asked to sleep for eight hours and then their test performance was compared with the population μ = 70%. For Study 2, a single sample of students was asked to sleep for eight hours before their first exam in a course and to stay up all night the night before their second exam in the course. For Study 3, students were randomly assigned to one of two groups: One group slept for eight hours the night before the exam and the other group stayed awake the night before the exam. For the table below, fill in the parts for each *t* test.

Test	When do you use this test?	Hypotheses H_0 & H_1			How do you run this test in SPSS?	Using SPSS, how do you know when to reject or fail to reject the H_0?
One-sample *t* FORMULA: Which study is this?		Two-tailed	One-tailed			
			IV ↑ DV	IV ↓ DV		
Paired samples *t* FORMULA: Which study is this?		Two-tailed	One-tailed			
			IV ↑ DV	IV ↓ DV		
Independent-sample *t* FORMULA: Which study is this?		Two-tailed	One-tailed			
			IV ↑ DV	IV ↓ DV		

37. Choose the Correct *t* Test

For each study description below, choose the correct inferential statistic to test the hypothesis.

(1) A single sample is recruited to study the effects of caffeine on work productivity. Each participant in the study completes a task in which they have to stack boxes on shelves for 15 minutes with and without caffeine. The researcher's hypothesis is that the participants will stack more boxes after drinking caffeine than without the caffeine.

    (a) One-tailed one-sample *t* test

    (b) Two-tailed one-sample *t* test

    (c) One-tailed paired samples *t* test

    (d) Two-tailed paired samples *t* test

(2) A researcher is interested in the connection between sleep and depression. A group of students is recruited for the study based on their scores on a depression questionnaire. Students with a score in the top 75th percentile of the population of scores on the scale are placed in the depressed group, and students with a score in the bottom 25th percentile of the population of scores on the scale are placed in the not depressed group. The researcher then asks the students to report the amount of sleep they have gotten on the past seven nights to compare the average number of sleep minutes per night across the two groups.

    (a) One-tailed independent samples *t* test

    (b) Two-tailed independent samples *t* test

    (c) One-tailed paired samples *t* test

    (d) Two-tailed paired samples *t* test

(3) The score on a standardized test in the population is known to be $\propto = 500$. A sample of students completes a new curriculum designed to increase the skills that the test measures. The mean and standard deviation of the students' scores on the test is calculated after the new curriculum has been administered.

    (a) One-tailed independent samples *t* test

    (b) Two-tailed independent samples *t* test

    (c) One-tailed one-sample *t* test

    (d) Two-tailed one-sample *t* test

(4) A developmental psychologist believes that working memory skills (i.e., the ability to keep track of multiple tasks at once) significantly increases between the ages of 5 and 8. She recruits children of these ages and gives them a working memory task to compare their scores.

    (a) One-tailed paired samples *t* test

    (b) Two-tailed paired samples *t* test

    (c) One-tailed independent samples *t* test

    (d) Two-tailed independent samples *t* test

(5) You think that quizzing yourself before a final exam will help you do better on the test than rereading your lecture notes but you are concerned that using yourself as a test

case will bias the results, so you recruit 10 of your friends who are willing to participate in your study to test your idea. Five of your friends say they reread their notes before tests and five of them say they quiz themselves before tests. You compare the final exam scores of your friends in each group to test your hypothesis.

(a) One-tailed one-sample t test

(b) One-tailed independent samples t test

(c) One-tailed paired samples t test

(d) None of the above

38. One-Way Between-Subjects ANOVA by Hand

A psychologist at a private mental hospital was asked to determine whether there was a clear difference in the length of stay for patients with different categories of diagnosis. Looking at the last four patients in each of the three major categories, the results (in terms of weeks of stay) were as follows:

Diagnosis Category		
Affective Disorders	Cognitive Disorders	Drug-Related Conditions
7	12	8
6	8	10
5	9	12
6	11	10

Using $\alpha = 0.05$, is there a significant difference in length of stay among diagnosis categories? Show all five steps of hypothesis testing.

39. One-Way Between-Subjects ANOVA in SPSS

1. Analyze the data below using SPSS.

Diagnosis Category		
Affective Disorders	Cognitive Disorders	Drug-Related Conditions
7	12	8
6	8	10
5	9	12
6	11	10

(a) Using SPSS (and $\alpha = 0.05$), is there a significant difference in length of stay among diagnosis categories? Compute the means and standard deviations for each group.

(b) Using Scheffe's test, find out which groups are different from each other.

2. Using the majors.sav data file (http://psychology.illinoisstate.edu/jccutti/StatsDataFiles/majors.sav), test whether there are differences in university grade point averages for different majors. Compute the means and standard deviations for each group. Conduct planned comparisons to test whether computer majors are different from engineering majors and computer majors from other sciences.

40. Factorial ANOVA

1. A sports psychologist studied the effect of a motivational program on the number of injuries in one year among players of three different sports. The chart below shows the design. For each of the following possible pattern of results, make up a set of cell means, complete the table with the missing condition means according the effect(s) listed, figure the marginal means, and make a bar graph of the results in the space at the right:

(a) a main effect for type of sport and no other main effect or interaction

	Sport		
	Baseball	Football	Basketball
With Motivational Program	5	7	9
Without Motivational Program			

(b) a main effect for program and no other main effect or interaction

	Sport		
	Baseball	Football	Basketball
With Motivational Program	5	5	5
Without Motivational Program			

(c) both main effects but no interaction

	Sport		
	Baseball	Football	Basketball
With Motivational Program	5	7	9
Without Motivational Program			

(d) no main effect for program or sport but an interaction

	Sport		
	Baseball	Football	Basketball
With Motivational Program	5	7	9
Without Motivational Program			

2. Carry out an analysis of variance for the following data set, including making a table of cell and marginal means and making a bar graph of the cell means. Use an alpha level of 0.05.

Participant	Level for IV_A	Level for IV_B	DV
A	1	1	9
B	1	1	7
C	1	2	3
D	1	2	1
E	2	1	1
F	2	1	3
G	2	2	7
H	2	2	9
I	3	1	1
J	3	1	3
K	3	2	7
L	3	2	9
M	4	1	9
N	4	1	7
O	4	2	3
P	4	2	1

3. Patients with two kinds of diagnoses were randomly assigned to one of three types of therapy. The table of data is presented below. There were two patients per cell. Use SPSS to compute the results listed below. Use an alpha level of 0.05.

(a) Carry out the analysis of variance.

(b) Compute the cell and marginal means.

(c) Make a graph of the results.

(d) Describe the results in words.

(e) Compute the effect size of the statistics.

	Therapy		
	A	B	C
Diagnosis I	6 2	3 1	2 4
Diagnosis II	11 9	7 9	8 10

4. When participants memorize a list of words serially (in the order of presentation), words at the beginning and end of the list are remembered better than words in the middle. This has been called the serial-position effect. You wonder whether this holds true across different presentation modalities (reading lists versus hearing lists). You give a group of four people two lists of words, one they heard read to them, the other they read to themselves. Then you look at the number of words recalled from the first part of the list, the middle part of the list, and the final part of the list. The data are as follows:

Heard			Read		
Start of list	*Middle of list*	*End of list*	*Start of list*	*Middle of list*	*End of list*
1	5	0	1	3	0
3	7	2	4	4	1
5	6	1	6	6	3
3	2	1	2	5	0

Is there a serial position effect for both methods? Are there main effects? Describe your results in a short paragraph that includes the relevant statistics, including descriptive statistics for conditions and levels of the independent variables. Assume an alpha level of 0.05.

5. For this problem, download and use the majors.sav data file (http://psychology.illinoisstate .edu/jccutti/StatsDataFiles/majors.sav).

    (a) Test whether university grade point average differs by gender and major. Describe the main effects and interactions (using means and a graph).

    (b) Examine whether there is an interaction between type of SAT test performance (math or verbal) and gender. Describe your results in a short paragraph.

41. One-Way Within-Subjects ANOVA

The following data were obtained from a research study examining the effect of sleep deprivation on motor skills performance. A sample of five participants was tested on a motor skills task after 24 hours of sleep deprivation, tested again after 36 hours, and tested once more after 48 hours. The dependent variable is the number of errors made on the motor skills task.

Participant	24 hours	36 hours	48 hours
A	0	1	5
B	0	0	0
C	1	3	5
D	0	1	5
E	4	5	9

Using an alpha level of 0.05, test whether these data indicate that the number of hours of sleep deprivation has a significant effect on motor skills performance. List all your steps of hypothesis testing.

42. One-Way Within-Subjects ANOVA in SPSS

1. Use SPSS to analyze the data below.

Participant	24 Hours	36 Hours	48 Hours
A	0	1	5
B	0	0	0
C	1	3	5
D	0	1	5
E	4	5	9

What can you conclude from your analysis?

2. It has been suggested that pupil size increases during emotional arousal. A researcher would, therefore, like to see whether the increase in pupil size is a function of the type of arousal (pleasant versus aversive). A random sample of five participants is selected for the study. Each participant views all three stimuli: neutral, pleasant, and aversive photographs. The neutral photograph portrays a plain brick building. The pleasant photograph consists of a young man and woman sharing a large ice cream cone. Finally, the aversive stimulus is a graphic photograph of an automobile accident. Upon viewing each stimulus, the pupil size is measured (in millimeters) with sophisticated equipment. The data are as follows. Test whether all groups are equal (assume an alpha level of 0.05):

Participant	Stimulus		
	Neutral	Pleasant	Aversive
A	4	8	3
B	3	6	3
C	2	5	2
D	3	3	6
E	3	8	1

3. Use the same data as above, but treat it as if the experimenters used a between-groups design (different groups for each stimulus type). How do the results differ from what you obtained in the situation above? Explain why this is. Which design leads to a statistically more powerful test?

Stimulus		
Neutral	Pleasant	Aversive
4	8	3
3	6	3
2	5	2
3	3	6
3	8	1

4. A human factors psychologist studied three computer keyboard designs. Three sample groups of individuals were given material to type on a particular keyboard, and the number of errors committed by each participant was recorded. Are the groups the same? Use both an ANOVA and Tukey post hoc test to answer this question. The data are as follows:

Keyboard A	Keyboard B	Keyboard C
0	6	6
4	8	5
0	5	9
1	4	4
0	2	6

43. ANOVA Review

For each of the following questions,

- identify which test to use,

- state your hypotheses,

- carry out the statistical test (either by hand or using SPSS), and

- make a decision about the null hypothesis (for all, assume that $\alpha = 0.05$).

(1) Suppose that for your senior research project, you decide to test the effectiveness of three different studying methods on learning. Method A is to have students only read the textbook but not go to class. Students assigned to Method B go to class and take notes but don't read the textbook. The Method C group doesn't read the textbook or go to class, they only get to look at another student's class notes.

Consider some data for our proposed experiment.

Study Method		
Book Alone	Taking Notes	Borrowing Notes
0	4	1
1	3	2
3	6	2
1	3	0
0	4	0

(2) Suppose that you are testing the long-term effects of a new memory drug. You (the researcher) believe that the drug should improve memory performance and that continued usage of the drug should lead to continued memory performance. You give a group of five individuals a pretest for memory. Then you have each start taking the new drug each week. After four weeks, you test their memory and then again after 16 weeks. The data are presented below. The scores are the number of items recalled in a memory test (out of a possible 10 items).

Person	Pretest	4-Week Test	16-Week Test
A	2	4	6
B	0	2	4
C	1	3	5
D	3	6	6
E	4	5	9

(3)   Consider the data from a 2×3 between-groups factorial design. There are six separate conditions, and each condition has five subjects in it ($N = 30$).

	B1	B2	B3
A1	5	9	3
	3	9	8
	3	13	3
	8	6	3
	6	8	3
A2	0	0	0
	2	0	3
	0	0	7
	0	5	5
	3	0	5

44. Which Test Should I Use?

For each study description below, choose the correct inferential statistic to test the hypothesis.

(1) A dietician is concerned that a new drug being sold to help people lose weight has a side effect of increased anxiety. He is especially concerned about high doses of the drug, which could cause very high levels of anxiety, prompting panic attacks in people who take too much of the drug. He recruits a sample of 90 people who want to lose weight. They are randomly assigned to one of three groups: the recommended drug dose group, the higher-than-recommended drug dose group, or the no-drug control group. The participants all receive an identical pill (with the control group's pill containing only sugar) to control for a placebo effect. After a period of three months, all the participants take a questionnaire to measure their anxiety levels. The scores for the three groups are compared.

(a) Independent samples t test

(b) One-way between-subjects ANOVA

(c) One-way within-subjects ANOVA

(d) Two-way ANOVA

(2) A cognitive psychologist thinks that carrying a heavy weight can change people's perception of the slope of hill they are asked to climb. Two groups of participants are asked to judge how steep they think a hill is on a 1 to 10 scale, with higher numbers indicating a higher level of steepness. One group wears a weighted backpack and the other group wears a backpack with no weights. The ratings of the hill are compared for the two groups.

(a) Paired samples t test

(b) Independent samples t test

(c) One-way ANOVA

(d) Two-way ANOVA

(3) A study has been conducted to compare men and women on the likelihood of seeking counseling for a psychological problem. A survey was completed by 1,000 men and 1,000 women to determine if they suffered more from anxiety or depression. The survey also asked participants to rate their likelihood of seeking counseling in the next six months on a 1 to 5 scale, with higher ratings indicating they were more likely to seek it. The likelihood ratings were compared for the conditions in the study to compare men and women, anxiety and depression groups, and the interaction between these factors.

(a) Paired samples t test

(b) Independent samples t test

(c) One-way ANOVA

(d) Two-way ANOVA

(4) To investigate whether playing video games increases hand–eye coordination, a game company conducts a study with a group of volunteers who all report having never played the company's games. Hand–eye coordination is measured at the start of the study. The participants are then asked to play the games for 25 hours per week for six weeks. Their hand–eye coordination is measured after the six-week period.

(a) Paired samples t test

(b) Independent samples t test

(c) One-way ANOVA

(d) Two-way ANOVA

45. Correlations and Scatterplots Exercise

1. Josie conducted an honors research project in which she measured IQ scores and the number of hours spent watching television per week for several students. Her results are shown below. Each pair of numbers represents one student; the IQ score is shown first and the number of hours of television watched per week is shown next (for both variables, a higher score means more).

   (a) On the graph shown, plot the data points for each student. Label each axis of the graph to indicate the variable plotted.

   (b) Below the graph, identify the relationship as either positive, negative, or no correlation.

   (c) Estimate the numerical correlation value (r) as a number between −1.0 and +1.0. Write your r estimate below the graph.

Scores

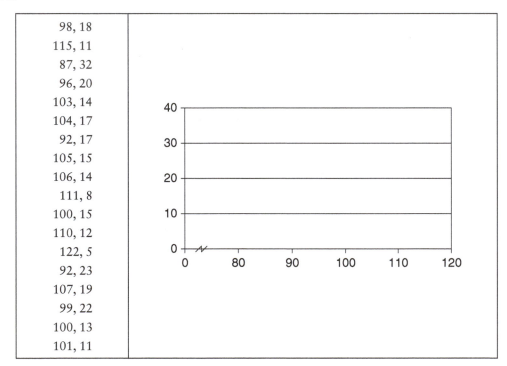

98, 18	
115, 11	
87, 32	
96, 20	
103, 14	
104, 17	
92, 17	
105, 15	
106, 14	
111, 8	
100, 15	
110, 12	
122, 5	
92, 23	
107, 19	
99, 22	
100, 13	
101, 11	

2. Each pair of variables below has a known relationship. Use common sense to determine what type of relationship likely exists between the variables.

   (a) The number of times per day you smile at other people and the number of times per day others smile at you

   (b) The number of hours per day a person studies and the number of exams per semester a person fails

   (c) The number of gallons of water a person drinks in a week and the number of close friends the person has

   (d) The number of alcoholic drinks a person has each week and their grade point average

46. Correlations and Scatterplots 2

1. Match the following graphs to the descriptions:

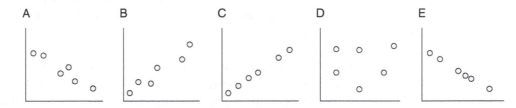

A   B   C   D   E

_____ Strong negative association

_____ Strong positive association

_____ Medium strength negative association

_____ Medium strength positive association

_____ No association

Computing a Pearson r (SS Formula)

2. Make a table that looks similar to the one below and complete the missing blanks (feel free to use a calculator).

	X	Y	$(X - \overline{X})$	$(Y - \overline{Y})$	$(X - \overline{X})(Y - \overline{Y})$	$(X - \overline{X})^2$	$(Y - \overline{Y})^2$
	0	1					
	10	3					
	4	1					
	8	2					
	8	3					
Sum	30	10					
Means	6	2					

Calculate the sum of products (SP), the sum of squared deviations for X (SS_x), the sum of squared deviations for Y (SS_y), and the Pearson correlation (r).

47. Correlations and Scatterplots in SPSS

Open the height.sav data file (http://psychology.illinoisstate.edu/jccutti/StatsDataFiles/height.sav). This fictional data set contains height, weight, age, and gender information for 40 individuals. Additionally, it has the average calcium intake (*calcium*), household income (*income*), and average parental height (*avgphgt*).

(1) Make scatterplots that plot the relationship between the response variable *height* and the three quantitative explanatory variables (*avgphgt, calcium, income*). For each scatterplot, describe the nature of the relationship (in terms of direction and strength).

(2) Make a scatterplot of height and weight and include gender as a categorical variable (mark the cases by gender). How does the relationship between height and weight compare for men and women?

(3) Compute a correlation matrix that computes the correlation coefficients between five of our variables (*height, weight, income, calcium, avgphgt*). Which variables have the strongest correlations? Which variables are negatively correlated?

48. Computing Correlations by Hand

1. Create a scatterplot based on the following data:

Person	Height	Average Parent Height
A	65 in	68 in
B	60 in	64 in
C	69 in	70 in
D	59 in	65 in
E	72 in	67 in
F	67 in	65 in

2. What is the direction of relationship (positive or negative) in this scatterplot? How strong of a relationship does there appear to be?

3. For the data above, find $\overline{X}$, $\overline{Y}$, s_x, s_y, SS_x, SS_y, and SP.

4. Now compute Pearson's correlation coefficient using the numbers found for SS_x, SS_y, and SP.

5. Interpret the r you just found. What is the direction and strength of the relationship? Does this match your interpretation based on the scatterplot?

49. Computing Correlations by Hand 2

You conduct a survey on how much your friends like a website and whether it is related to their grade point average (GPA). Your survey's response scale runs from 0 = *do not like at all* to 5 = *absolutely love*. Your assignment is to provide all descriptive statistics for the following data set.

Person	Web Liking	GPA
A	5	2.4
B	1	3.9
C	2	3.5
D	4	2.8
E	3	3.0

Person	Web Liking	GPA
F	2	2.1
G	4	3.9
H	3	2.9
I	0	3.6
J	3	2.7

(1) Make a scatterplot of both of your variables by entering the letter of each person on the proper place on the graph. Draw the best-fit line through the set of points.

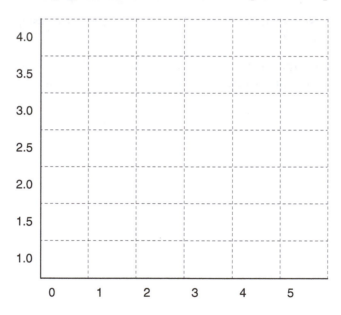

(2) Find the following statistics for Xs and Ys for the data above. Show formulas and calculations.

$$\qquad\qquad\qquad\qquad\qquad\qquad\qquad X \qquad\quad Y$$

$$Mode =$$

$$Median =$$

$$Range =$$

$$M =$$

$$SS =$$

$$Variance =$$

$$SD =$$

Find the following statistic for Xs and Ys together. Show formulas and calculations.

$$Pearson\ r =$$

50. Hypothesis Testing With Correlation

Show all four steps of hypothesis testing in your answer (some questions will require more for each step than others) and be sure to state hypotheses in terms of ρ.

(1) A high school counselor would like to know if there is a relationship between mathematical skill and verbal skill. A sample of $n = 25$ students is selected, and the counselor records achievement test scores in mathematics and English for each student. The Pearson correlation for this sample is $r = +0.50$. Do these data provide sufficient evidence for a real relationship in the population? Use a two-tailed test with $\alpha = 0.05$.

(2) It is well known that similarity in attitudes, beliefs, and interests plays an important role in interpersonal attraction. Thus, correlations for attitudes between married couples should be strong and positive. Suppose a researcher developed a questionnaire that measures how liberal or conservative one's attitudes is. Low scores indicate that the person has liberal attitudes while high scores indicate conservatism. Here are the data from the study:

     Couple A: Husband 14, Wife 11

     Couple B: Husband 7, Wife 6

     Couple C: Husband 15, Wife 18

     Couple D: Husband 7, Wife 4

     Couple E: Husband 3, Wife 1

     Couple F: Husband 9, Wife 10

     Couple G: Husband 9, Wife 5

     Couple H: Husband 3, Wife 3

     Test the researcher's hypothesis with $\alpha = 0.05$.

(3) A researcher believes that a person's belief in supernatural events (e.g., ghosts, extrasensory perception, etc.) is related to their education level. For a sample of $n = 30$ people, he gives them a questionnaire that measures their belief in supernatural events (a high score means they believe in more of these events) and asks them how many years of schooling they've had. He finds that $SS_{beliefs} = 10$, $SS_{schooling} = 10$, and $SP = -8$. With $\alpha = 0.01$, test the researcher's hypothesis.

51. Hypothesis Testing With Correlation Using SPSS

To measure the relationship between anxiety and test performance, a researcher asked his students to come to the lab 15 minutes before they were to take an exam in his class. The researcher measured the students' heart rates and then matched these scores with their exam performance after they had taken the exam. Use the data below and SPSS to conduct a hypothesis test for the correlation between anxiety and test performance in the population. Use $\alpha = 0.05$.

Student	Heart Rate	Exam Score
A	76	78
B	81	68
C	60	88
D	65	80
E	80	90
F	66	68
G	82	60
H	71	95
I	66	84
J	75	75
K	80	62
L	76	51
M	77	63
N	79	71

52. Regression

1. A set of X and Y scores have a mean of X of 4, SS_x of 15, mean of Y of 5, and SP of 30.

   (a) What is the regression equation for predicting Y from X?

   (b) What are the predicted Y scores for the following X scores: 3, –2, 5, 6.

2. Find the regression equation for predicting Y from X for the following set of scores. (Show your work for each step.)

X	Y
0	9
1	7
2	11

3. Find the regression equation and standard error of estimate for the following set of data. (Show your work for each step.)

X	Y
4	1
7	16
3	4
5	7
6	7

4. When a correlation is close to ±1.0, then the standard error of the estimate will be _____. When the correlation is close to 0, then the standard error of estimate will be _____.

   (a) large, small

   (b) close to 1.0, close to 0

   (c) small, large

   (d) cannot tell from the information given

53. Chi-Square Test for Independence

1. New research seems to suggest that kids raised in homes with pets tend to have fewer allergies than kids raised without pets. A survey study was conducted to test this finding. A sample of 100 adults were asked if they had allergies (yes/no) and how many pets they had between the ages of 1 and 10 years old (0, 1, or 2 or more). Use the crosstabs table below to conduct a chi-square test with $\alpha = 0.05$. Indicate whether these data support the previous findings or not.

# Pets/Allergies	0	1	2 or more
No	10	25	35
Yes	15	10	5

2. For the following voting survey data, create a crosstabs table and then conduct a test to determine if the two variables are related. Use $\alpha = 0.01$.

Person	Gender	Plans to Vote for	Person	Gender	Plans to Vote for
1	Male	Trump	16	Female	Clinton
2	Male	Trump	17	Male	Trump
3	Female	Trump	18	Male	Clinton
4	Female	Clinton	19	Female	Trump
5	Female	Clinton	20	Female	Trump
6	Male	Clinton	21	Male	Clinton
7	Male	Trump	22	Female	Clinton
8	Female	Clinton	23	Male	Trump
9	Female	Trump	24	Female	Clinton
10	Male	Clinton	25	Female	Trump
11	Male	Trump	26	Male	Trump
12	Female	Trump	27	Female	Clinton
13	Male	Clinton	28	Male	Trump
14	Female	Clinton	29	Female	Clinton
15	Male	Trump	30	Male	Trump

SECTION 2

Meet the Formulae

This section of the lab manual will include exercises that break down selected formulae to allow students to better understand their underlying conceptual components and to recognize the similarities and differences between formulae by virtue of how they often share these components. These can be done as individual or group exercises.

54. Meet the Formula: Standard Deviation

Variance and standard deviation are calculated a little differently, depending on whether you are measuring a population distribution or a sample distribution. Since most of the time we are dealing with data from a sample, we will discuss how to compute the standard deviation from a sample. Standard deviation is most frequently reported for a set of scores because it is a more intuitive value, but you'll see later that we can use the variance to calculate some statistical values.

The complete formula is as follows:

$$standard\,deviation\,(sample) = \sqrt{\frac{\Sigma(X - \overline{X})^2}{n - 1}}$$

Use the following formula:

Step 1: Compute the sample mean.

Step 2: Compute the deviation scores and sum of squares (*SS*).

Step 3: Determine the variance of the sample.

Step 4: Determine the standard deviation of the sample.

Suppose we have the following set of sample scores: 1, 2, 3, 4, 5. Remember that the standard deviation measures how far off all of the scores in a distribution are from the mean (the mean is used to represent the standard score within a distribution).

1.   Compute the mean for this sample. This is the $\overline{X}$ in the formula.

   (a) Why is the sample mean a good standard for the sample?

The next step is to find the deviation scores. These are calculated by subtracting the mean from each score. This corresponds to the $(X - \overline{X})$ part of the formula. Each deviation score tells us how far the score is from the mean.

2.   Complete the table below by computing the deviation scores for each score in the sample.

Score	Deviation
X	$(X - \overline{X})$
5	5–3 =
4	4–3 =
3	3–3 =
2	2–3 =
1	1–3 =

   (a) Why must the scores sum to zero?

Next, you square all the deviations. This must be done because simply adding all the deviations together will equal out to zero. This is because you are taking one side of the distribution and making it positive and making the other side negative. Thus, they will cancel each other out. To get rid of the positive and negative signs, we square the deviations and add them up. The final result is the called the *sum of squared deviation scores* or, more commonly, the *sum of squares* (SS).

Sum of squares: $SS = \sum\left(X - \overline{X}\right)^2$

3. Compute the *SS* for this sample.

    (a) Is it possible to end up with a negative value for *SS*?

The next step is to find the variance, which is essentially the average of the squared deviations. To get this average, we need to divide the *SS* by the number of scores in the sample ($n - 1$). The symbol for the sample variance is s^2 (another notation is *SD*). We divide by $n - 1$ instead of n to correct for the fact that samples tend to be less variable than the populations from which they are drawn. In most cases, we are using the sample standard deviation as an estimate of the population standard deviation.

Variance for a sample: $s^2 = \dfrac{SS}{(n-1)}$

4. Compute the variance for this sample.

    (a) Consider why your value of variance is too high to be considered the average deviation in the sample.

To get the standard deviation, we need to correct for all the squared deviation by taking the square root of the population variance. Thus, the standard deviation is the square root of the mean squared deviation.

Standard deviation (sample): $s = \sqrt{s^2} = \sqrt{\dfrac{\sum\left(X - \overline{X}\right)^2}{n-1}}$

5. Compute the standard deviation for this sample.

    (a) How would you explain standard deviation to somebody who doesn't know what it is?

55. Meet the Formula: *z* Score Transformation

Transforming a raw score into a *z* score is useful for locating a score in a distribution and is especially useful for comparing scores from different distributions.

The formula is this:

$$z - score = \frac{X - \mu}{\sigma}$$

Use the following steps:

Step 1: Compute the deviation score (score minus the mean).

Step 2: Divide by the standard deviation.

The resulting transformed score has the following properties:

- The direction is indicated by the negative or positive sign on the deviation score.

- The distance from the mean is the value of the deviation score.

Suppose that you are a 5'7" tall male who weighs 180 lbs. You want to know if you weigh more than you should, given that you consider yourself somewhat short. Comparing your weight and height can be difficult because the two are measured on different scales. You can use *z* scores to directly compare the two scores. Suppose that for men over the age of 20 in the United States, the mean height is 69 inches (*SD* = 3) and the mean weight is 190 lbs. (*SD* = 36).

Step 1: Compute the deviation score for height. Do the same for weight.

(a) For each, is your deviation score above or below the mean? Can you easily tell if you are comparatively heavy for your weight? Why or why not?

Step 2: Divide the each of your deviation scores by their standard deviations.

(a) Compare how much you differ from the averages for height and weight in terms of *z* scores. Is it easier to make a conclusion about whether you are too heavy? How does transforming the raw scores into standardized *z* scores help make the comparison?

56. Meet the Formula: Single-Sample z Tests and t Tests

Single-sample z tests and t tests are used when comparing single samples to the mean of a known population of samples. The two formulae are very similar to one another.

The formulae are as follows:

Single-Sample z Test	Single-Sample t Test
$z = \dfrac{\overline{X} - \mu}{\sigma_{\overline{X}}}$	$t = \dfrac{\overline{X} - \mu}{s_{\overline{X}}}$
$\sigma_{\overline{X}} = \dfrac{\sigma}{\sqrt{n}}$	$s_{\overline{X}} = \dfrac{s}{\sqrt{n}}$

Complete the following steps by using the formulae above:

Step 1: Compute the deviation score (the sample mean minus the population mean).

Step 2: Compute the either the standard error or the estimated standard error.

Step 3: Divide the deviation score by the standard error or the estimated standard error.

1. Compare the single-sample z test formula with the z score formula used to locate a single score in a distribution. How are the formulae similar and how do they differ?

2. Compare the single-sample z test formula with the single-sample t test formula. How are these formulae similar and how do they differ?

3. Suppose that you took a standardized test with a mean of 500 and a standard deviation of 100.

   (a) If you received a score of 630 on the test, what is the probability of getting that score or better?

   (b) Suppose that you and a group of your three friends scored 670, 570, 690, and 590 on the test. What is the probability of getting the mean of these scores or better?

   (c) Suppose that you and a group of your three friends scored 670, 570, 690, and 590 on the test, but you don't know the population standard deviation. (Hint: This means you cannot calculate a z score for the mean.) Is the probability of getting the sample mean for these scores greater than 0.05 or not?

   (d) How do the three different scenarios above compare with each other? Examine the components of the formulae. How do the numerators compare? How do the denominators compare?

57. Meet the Formula: Comparing Independent Samples and Related Samples t Tests

The formula that is used to compare two groups depends on the assumptions of the designs used to generate the data. If the two groups are composed of independent observations, then an independent samples t test is used. However, if the two groups of observations are related, then the related samples t test is used.

The formulae are as follows:

Independent Samples t Test	Related Samples t Test
$t = \dfrac{\left(\overline{X}_A - \overline{X}_B\right) - \left(\mu_A - \mu_B\right)}{s_{\overline{X}_A - \overline{X}_B}}$	$t = \dfrac{\overline{D} - \mu_D}{s_{\overline{D}}}$
$s_{\overline{X}_A - \overline{X}_B} = \sqrt{\dfrac{s_p^2}{n_A} + \dfrac{s_p^2}{n_B}}$	$s_{\overline{D}} = \dfrac{s_D}{\sqrt{n}}$
$s_p^2 = \dfrac{SS_A + SS_B}{df_A + df_B}$	$s_D = \sqrt{\dfrac{SS_D}{n-1}} = \sqrt{\dfrac{\left(D - \overline{D}\right)^2}{n-1}}$

1. Compare the numerator portion of the two t tests.

   (a) How are the $\left(\overline{X}_A - \overline{X}_B\right)$ and $\overline{D}$ parts of the formulae similar? How are they different?

   (b) How are the $\left(\mu_A - \mu_B\right)$ and the μ_D parts of the formulae similar? How are they different?

2. Compare the denominator portion of the two t tests.

   (a) How are the two estimated standard errors $(s_{\overline{X}_A - \overline{X}_B}$ and $s_{\overline{D}})$ similar and how are they different? Why does the independence of the two groups of observations lead to these differences?

   (b) How are the variance formulae $(s_p^2$ and $s_D)$ similar and different? Why does the independence of the two groups of observations lead to these differences?

3. Consider the following set of data:

Group A	Group B
45	43
55	49
40	35
60	51

   (a) Analyze the data, assuming that the two groups of observations are independent.

   (b) Analyze the data, assuming that the two groups of observations are related.

   (c) Explain why the conclusions that you drew above are different, given that the numbers that you start with are identical.

58. Meet the Formula: One-Factor Between-Subjects ANOVA

Suppose that you want to see if there is an effect of an independent variable with three between-subjects levels. Consider the data below.

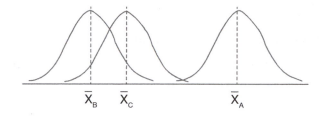

$$\overline{X}_B \quad \overline{X}_C \qquad \qquad \overline{X}_A$$

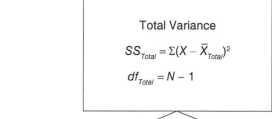

Total Variance

$$SS_{Total} = \Sigma(X - \overline{X}_{Total})^2$$

$$df_{Total} = N - 1$$

Between Groups Variance

$$SS_{Between} = n\Sigma(\overline{X}_{Group} - \overline{X}_{Total})^2$$

$$df_{Between} = a - 1$$

$$MS_{Between} = \frac{SS_{Between}}{df_{Between}}$$

Within Groups Variance

$$SS_{Within} = \Sigma(SS_{Group})$$

$$df_{Within} = a(n - 1)$$

$$MS_{Within} = \frac{SS_{Within}}{df_{Within}}$$

Group A	Group B	Group C
10	5	4
7	1	6
5	3	9
10	7	3
8	4	3

ANOVA stands for analysis of variance. The goal of this procedure is to partition the total overall variance into two components: variance coming from within each group and variance coming from between each of the groups. Essentially, the process is similar to that used when computing variance and standard deviation. However, instead of doing that for one group, here, variance is considered with several different groupings.

Use the steps below to compute the total variance (for the entire set of observations):

Step 1: Compute the grand mean ($\overline{X}_{Grand}$) (add up all the scores and divide by the total number of scores).

Step 2: Compute the SS_{Total} (find the deviation scores [subtract the grand mean from each score], square the deviation scores, and add all the deviation scores together).

Step 3: Compute the df_{Total} (the total number of scores minus one).

Step 4: Compute the MS_{Total} (total variance).

(1) Compare this step with the steps used earlier for computing variance and standard deviation. What are the similarities and the differences?

Use the following steps for computing within-groups variance (variance for Group A, B, and C separately):

Step 1: Compute the mean of each group (A, B, and C).

Step 2: Compute the SS for each group (for each group separately, find the deviation scores, square the deviation scores, and add all the deviation scores together).

Step 3: Compute the df_{group} for each group (the number of scores in the group minus one).

Step 4: Compute the SS_{Within} (add up the SS from each group).

Step 5: Compute the df_{Within} (add up the df from each group).

Step 6: Compute the MS_{Within} (divide the SS_{Within} by the df_{Within}).

(2) Compare this step with the steps used earlier for computing variance and standard deviation. What are the similarities and the differences?

Use the steps below to compute the between-groups variance (for across Groups A, B, and C):

Step 1: Compute the mean of each group (A, B, and C).

Step 2: Compute the SS for between groups ($SS_{Between}$) (find the deviation scores between the group means and the grand mean [GM], square the deviation scores, weight the deviation scores by the number of scores in the group, and add all the weighted deviation scores together).

Step 3: Compute the $df_{Between}$ (the number of groups minus one).

Step 4: Compute the $MS_{Between}$ (divide the $SS_{Between}$ by the $df_{Between}$).

    (3)   Compare this step with the steps used earlier for computing variance and standard deviation. What are the similarities and the differences?

Use the steps below to compute the F ratio:

Step 1: Compare the between-groups variance with the within-groups variance (divide the $MS_{Between}$ by the MS_{Within}).

    (4)   How is the F ratio similar to the final ratio used in the independent samples t test?

59. Meet the Formula: Two-Factor ANOVA

Suppose that you want to see if there are effects of two separate independent variables tested in the same experimental design. The analysis that you can do is a two-factor analysis of variance (ANOVA). In addition to testing the effects of each of the independent variables, the factorial ANOVA will also allow you to test whether the two variables also interact with each other. Consider the data below.

		Factor B		
		B_1	B_2	B_3
Factor A	A_1	3	2	0
		1	5	0
		1	9	4
		6	7	3
		4	7	1
	A_2	3	3	0
		0	8	0
		0	3	0
		2	3	5
		0	3	0

The goal of this procedure is to partition the total overall variance into two components: variance coming from within each group and variance coming from between each of the groups. Essentially, the process is similar to that used to compute variance and standard deviation. However, instead of doing that for one group, here, variance is considered with several different groupings. The first partition that is made is the same as that used for the one factor between-subjects ANOVA analysis. However, because there is more than one independent variable, the variability is further partitioned in additional ways.

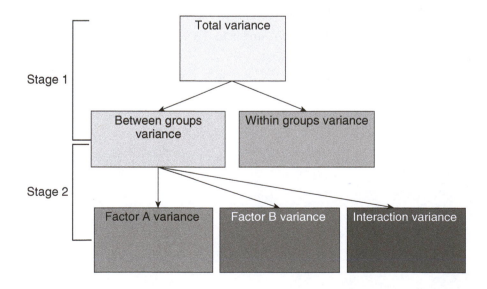

$$SS_{Total} = \Sigma\left(X - \overline{X}_{Grand}\right)^2 \qquad df_{Total} = N - 1 \qquad MS_{Total} = \frac{SS_{Total}}{df_{Total}}$$

Use the steps below to compute total variance (for the entire set of observations):

Step 1: Compute the grand mean (*GM*) (add up all the scores and divide by the total number of scores).

Step 2: Compute the SS_{Total} (find the deviation scores [subtract the *GM* from each score], square the deviation scores, and add all the deviation scores together).

Step 3: Compute the df_{Total} (the total number of scores minus one).

Step 4: Compute the MS_{Total} (total variance).

    (1)   Compare this step with the steps used earlier for computing total variance in the one-factor ANOVA analysis.

$$SS_{Within} = \Sigma\left(X - \overline{X}_{AB}\right)^2 \qquad df_{Within} = (a)*(b)(n-1) \qquad MS_{Within} = \frac{SS_{Within}}{df_{within}}$$

Use the steps below to compute within-groups variance (for each of the conditions, all six groups):

Step 1: Compute the mean of each group.

Step 2: Compute the *SS* for each group separately (find the deviation scores, square the deviation scores, and add all the deviation scores together).

Step 3: Compute the SS_{Within} (compute the *SS* for each condition separately and then add up the *SS* from each group).

Step 4: Compute the df_{Within} (multiply the number of levels of A by the number of levels of B by the number of participants in each condition).

Step 5: Compute the MS_{Within} (divide the SS_{Within} by the df_{Within}).

(2) Compare this step with the steps used earlier for computing the within-groups variance in the one-factor ANOVA analysis?

$$SS_A = n(b)\sum\left(\overline{X}_A - \overline{X}_{Grand}\right)^2 \qquad df_A = a - 1 \qquad MS_A = \frac{SS_{Within}}{df_{within}}$$

$$SS_B = n(a)\sum\left(\overline{X}_B - \overline{X}_{Grand}\right)^2 \qquad df_B = b - 1 \qquad MS_B = \frac{SS_{Within}}{df_{within}}$$

$$SS_{AB} = n\sum\left(\overline{X}_{AB} - \overline{X}_A - \overline{X}_B + \overline{X}_{Grand}\right)^2 \qquad df_{AB} = (a)*(b)(n-1) \qquad MS_{AB} = \frac{SS_{Within}}{df_{within}}$$

Use the following steps to partition the between-groups variance into main effect and interaction components:

Main Effect of A

Step 1: Compute the marginal mean of each level of each variable (across the columns).

Step 2: Compute the SS_A (find the deviation scores between the means of the levels of A and the grand mean [$\overline{X}_{Grand}$], square the deviation scores, weight the deviation scores by the number of scores in the group and the number of levels of B, and add all the weighted deviation scores together).

Step 3: Compute the df_A (the number of levels minus one).

Step 4: Compute the MS_A (divide the SS_A by the df_A).

Main Effect of B

For the main effect of B repeat the steps above but for the B conditions instead of A (so use the marginal means down the columns).

Interaction

Step 1: Use marginal means for A and B (from the main effects steps).

Step 2: Compute the SS_{AB}. The deviation scores are more complex here. In each condition, subtract the corresponding marginal mean of both A ($\overline{X}_A$) and B ($\overline{X}_B$) from the condition mean ($\overline{X}_{AB}$). Then add the grand mean ($\overline{X}_{Grand}$). Square the deviation scores, add all the weighted deviation scores together, and weight the deviation scores by the number of scores in each condition.

Step 3: Compute the df_{AB} (multiply the number of levels of A − 1, the number of levels of B − 1, and n − 1).

Step 4: Compute the MS_A (divide the SS_{AB} by the df_{AB}).

> (3) How do the deviation scores used in the main effects of A and B compare with the steps used earlier for computing variance and standard deviation. What are the similarities and the differences?

Use the following steps to compute the F ratio:

Step 1: Compare the main effect and interaction variance components with the within-groups variance.

Step 2: For the main effect of A, divide the MS_A by the MS_{Within}.

Step 3: For the main effect of B divide MS_B by the MS_{Within}.

Step 4: For the interaction of A and B, divide the MS_{AB} by the MS_{Within}.

> (4) How are the three F ratios similar to each other? How are they different?

60. Meet the Formula: One-Factor Within-Subjects ANOVA

Suppose that you want to see if there is an effect of an independent variable with three within-subjects levels. Consider the data below.

Group A	Group B	Group C
3	4	6
0	3	3
2	1	4
0	1	3
0	1	4

Here is the partitioning of the variance for this design that is needed to calculate the F ratio:

$$SS_{Between} = n\Sigma\left(\overline{X}_A - \overline{X}_{Grand}\right)^2 \qquad df_{Between} = a - 1 \qquad MS_{Between} = \frac{SS_{Between}}{df_{Between}}$$

$$SS_{Within} = n\Sigma\left(\overline{X}_{AB} - \overline{X}_A - \overline{X}_B + \overline{X}_{Grand}\right)^2 \qquad df_{Error} = a - 1 \qquad MS_{Error} = \frac{SS_{Error}}{df_{Error}}$$

$$F - ratio = \frac{MS_{Between}}{MS_{Error}}$$

Recall that for a within-subjects design, there must be the same number of observations in each of the levels of the independent variable. This is because each participant experiences each condition of the study. In the df formula, a is the number of levels of the independent variable (in our example, we have three conditions).

1. Compare the $SS_{Between}$ formula for the one-factor between-subjects ANOVA with the formula for a one-factor within-subjects ANOVA. Why can the n be moved outside of the summation in the between-groups variance formula for this data set?

Recall that an interaction tells us if the differences across the levels of one factor are the same or different for each level of the other factor (i.e., does the effect of one factor depend on the level of the other factor?). Here, one of our factors is the subject, where each subject is a different level. We expect the subjects as a whole to differ across the conditions if the independent variable has an effect. But when the subjects show varying differences from one another across the conditions (i.e., an interaction between the subjects and the conditions), this represents the error we get from subject to subject in our study. Thus, we will use the interaction term as our error term because the interaction between the subjects and the conditions will give us an estimate of the error that exists in our data based on differences from subject to subject across the conditions of the study.

2. Compare the within-groups variance formula for the within-subjects design with the between-groups variance formula for the interaction in the factorial between-subjects design. How do the formulae differ? Why are subjects considered a factor in the within-groups variance term for this design?

61. Meet the Formula: Correlation

Computing the correlation between two continuous variables involves investigating how the scores on the two variables move relative to their standards and each other.

The formula is this:

$$r = \frac{SP}{SS_X SS_Y} = \frac{\Sigma\left(X - \overline{X}\right)\left(Y - \overline{Y}\right)}{\sqrt{\Sigma\left(X - \overline{X}\right)^2 \Sigma\left(Y - \overline{Y}\right)^2}}$$

Step 1: Compute the deviation scores for X and Y.

Step 2: Compute the sum of the products (SP), multiply the deviation score of X and Y for each observation and then add them all together.

Step 3: Compute the sum of the squared deviations (SS) for X and for Y, add up all of the squared deviation scores for X, repeat for Y.

Step 4: Multiply the SS_X and SS_Y.

Step 5: Divide the SP with the product of SS_X and SS_Y.

1. Consider the small data set below.

Person	X	Y
A	6	7
B	5	6
C	3	4
D	2	3
E	4	5

(a) Using the axes to the right of the table, make a scatterplot of X and Y. Based on your scatterplot, what value of r do you expect?

(b) Using the steps outlined above, compute r.

(c) Examine the deviation scores that you used to compute the SP in the numerator. What do you notice about their signs (+ and −)?

2. Consider the small data set below.

Person	X	Y
A	6	4
B	5	3
C	3	1
D	4	2
E	7	5

(a) Using the axes to the right of the table, make a scatterplot of X and Y. Based on your scatterplot, what value of r do you expect?

(b) Using the steps outlined above, compute r.

(c) Examine the deviation scores that you used to compute the *SP* in the numerator. What do you notice about their signs (+ and –)?

(d) What does a $r = -1.0$ or $r = +1.0$ mean about how the numerator and the denominator of the ratio? What does this suggest about how the covariance between *X* and *Y* compares with the product of how *X* and *Y* vary?

3. Consider the small data set below.

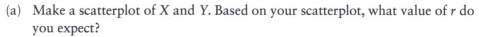

Person	X	Y
A	6	3
B	5	4
C	3	4
D	2	5

(a) Make a scatterplot of *X* and *Y*. Based on your scatterplot, what value of *r* do you expect?

(b) Imagine that the calculated *r* for this data set equals zero. What value would you expect in the numerator of the formula for *r* with this result?

62. Meet the Formula: Bivariate Regression

The computation of the components of bivariate regression shares many similarities with the computations used for correlation. Scatterplots are useful graphs for visualizing both correlation and regression analyses. The regression analysis results in computing the slope and intercept of the best-fit line that characterizes the relationship between the two variables being compared.

Consider the small data set below.

Person	X	Y
A	6	7
B	5	6
C	3	4
D	2	3
E	4	5

1. Using the axes to the right of the table, make a scatterplot of X and Y. Draw a line through the points that you think fit best. Note where the line crosses the Y axis.

Regression

$$slope = b = \frac{SP}{SS_X} = \frac{\Sigma\left(X-\overline{X}\right)\left(Y-\overline{Y}\right)}{\sqrt{\Sigma\left(X-\overline{X}\right)^2}}$$

$$intercept = a = \overline{Y} - b\overline{X}$$

Correlation

$$r = \frac{SP}{SS_X SS_Y} = \frac{\Sigma\left(X-\overline{X}\right)\left(Y-\overline{Y}\right)}{\sqrt{\Sigma\left(X-\overline{X}\right)^2 \Sigma\left(Y-\overline{Y}\right)^2}}$$

(a) Using the steps outlined above, compute the slope and intercept for the best-fit line. Plot that line on your scatterplot. How does it compare to your estimated line?

(b) On your scatterplot, indicate a point that corresponds to $\overline{X}$ and $\overline{Y}$. Does it fall on the line that you computed?

(c) Examine the deviation scores that you used to compute the SP in the numerator in your slope computation. What do you notice about their signs (+ and −)?

(d) Compare the formula for the slope with the formula for the correlation. How are they similar to and different from each other?

SECTION 3

Data Analysis Projects

This section of the lab manual includes data sets that students can use to complete data analysis projects. Some data sets are downloadable sets that correspond to the design of a published study. In addition, some activities in this section are designed to help students complete different steps in the analysis project (e.g., choose the correct test and run the analysis, interpret the analysis). Other activities are designed as a culminating project, asking students to complete all steps of the analysis in one activity. Downloadable data sets accompany this section of the lab manual to allow use in computer software packages.

63. Data Analysis Exercise: von Hippel, Ronay, Baker, Kjelsaas, and Murphy (2016)

Use the description below of this study to conduct the appropriate data analysis and answer the questions below. Data are available for download from https://osf.io/dfm8r/

Purpose of the Study. In this study, the researchers explored possible cognitive abilities that are related to social skills and one's charisma. In particular, they examined whether one's mental speed could predict social skills related to social comfort, conflict, and interpreting others' feelings. They also tested whether one's mental speed could predict how charismatic, funny, and quick-witted one was.

Method of the Study. Two studies were conducted. Each study included 200 participants comprised of groups of friends. In Study 1, participants completed an intelligence test (control measure), a five-factor personality survey (control measure), and 30 general knowledge questions (e.g., "Name a precious gem."). General knowledge questions provided the measure of mental speed, as participants were asked to answer the questions aloud as quickly as possible and their time to answer was measured on each question. Participants also completed three-item surveys for both social skills and charisma, rating each person in their friend group on a 1 to 7 scale. In Study 2, the participants completed the same general knowledge questions, social skills and charisma ratings, and personality survey as in Study 1. In addition, participants in Study 2 also completed speeded left–right dot detection and pattern-matching tasks as measures of mental speed, and surveys for self-control, self-efficacy (i.e., self-esteem), narcissism, social values, and self-confidence as control measures.

(1) List the independent and dependent variables in these studies.

(2) Were these studies experiments or correlational studies? Explain your answer.

(3) Based on the stated purpose and the type of data collected, what is the appropriate statistical test for the data from these studies?

(4) Download the data for the study and conduct the hypothesis tests for Study 1 and 2. What conclusions should the authors have made from these results?

(5) Download the article using the reference below. Take a look at the results for each study that correspond to the analyses you did (you can ignore other parts of their results that are more complicated and beyond the scope of this exercise). Did your results and conclusions match theirs? Why or why not?

von Hippel, W., Ronay, R., Baker, E., Kjelsaas, K., & Murphy, S. C. (2016). Quick thinkers are smooth talkers: Mental speed facilitates charisma. *Psychological Science, 27,* 119–122.

64. Data Analysis Exercise: Nairne, Pandeirada, and Thompson (2008)

Use the description below of this study to conduct the appropriate data analysis and answer the questions below. Data for the exercise are available for download from https://osf.io/4nd8g/

Purpose of the Study. In this study, the researchers examined the effect of survival processing on later memory. They hypothesized that if information is processed according to its survival relevance when studied, later memory for the information would be enhanced based on the adaptive value of memory.

Method of the Study. Participants were presented with words to rate one at a time. For some words, they rated the word's relevance to surviving (S) if you were lost in the grasslands and had to find food, water, and shelter. For other words, they had to rate the word's relevance to going on vacation (V) to a fancy resort where you had to find activities to do and organize your time. Words were presented in blocks of eight words for each rating task and each ratings task was presented twice. The order of the blocks was counterbalanced across participants (SVSV or VSVS). Ratings were made on a 1 to 5 scale, where higher ratings indicated higher relevance. After the fourth block of words, participants completed a short distractor task and then were given a surprise recall test for all of the words presented. The data file contains the counterbalancing condition, mean rating for each study task, mean percentage recall of words for each study task, and the mean response time for rating the words for each study task for each participant.

(1) List the independent and dependent variables in this study.

(2) Was this study an experiment or correlational study? Explain your answer.

(3) Based on the stated purpose and the type of data collected, what is the appropriate statistical test for the data from this study?

(4) Download the data for the study and conduct the hypothesis tests for this study. What conclusions should the authors have made from these results?

(5) The data you analyzed are from the Reproducibility Project to replicate Experiment 2 of the Nairne et al. (2008) study. Download the article using the reference below. Take a look at the results for Experiment 2 from the article and compare them to the analyses you did. Did your results and conclusions match theirs? Why or why not?

Nairne, J. S., Pandeirada, J. N. S., & Thompson, S. R. (2008). Adaptive memory: The comparative value of survival processing. *Psychological Science, 19,* 176–180.

65. Data Analysis Project 1: Crammed Versus Distributed Study

Use the description below of this study and the data set indicated to answer the research questions listed. You will need to use both descriptive and inferential statistics to complete this project. You can download the SPSS data file Analysis_project_1.sav from http://psychology .illinoisstate.edu/jccutti/StatsDataFiles/Analysis_project_1.sav for the analyses. Write an APA-style results section based on the analyses you conducted.

Research Project Description

The data for your project is the result of an organizational study of the effectiveness of a communication skills training program. Thirty management employees from the XYZ Corporation were interested in improving their group communication skills. These employees signed up for a 12-week "Group Communication and You" training course. An additional 30 management employees who were not interesting in completing the training course served as a control/comparison group.

All employees were observed as they interacted in group settings prior to the training period. Observers recorded scores of employees' communication skills on a scale that ranged from 0 to 50 (with higher scores indicating better communication skills). After the 12-week training period (or, for the untrained group, after 12 weeks had passed), all employees were observed again and their communication effectiveness was rated using the same scale.

The researchers also measured employees' extraversion. *Extraversion* is defined as the extent to which individuals are outgoing, assertive, and sociable (high extraversion) versus reserved, timid, and quiet (low extraversion). This measure was given to all employees prior to the 12-week training period because the researchers suspected that extraversion may be related to one's communication effectiveness.

The researchers (pretend that's you) are interested in several things:

- Is there a difference in communication skills at Time 2 between the trained and untrained groups?

- Did the trained group improve their communication skills after the training (Time 1 versus Time 2)?

- Is extraversion related to communication skills?

Data Set Details

- **subject:** This refers to the subject number assigned to each subject. Each row corresponds to one subject's data.

- **traingp:** This variable refers to whether the employee is in the trained or untrained group (0 = untrained, 1 = trained).

- **extrav:** This variable refers to the extraversion score of each subject.

- **time1:** This variable refers to the subjects' communication effectiveness scores prior to the 12-week period.

- **time2:** This variable refers to the subjects' communication effectiveness scores after the 12-week training period

66. Data Analysis Project 2: Teaching Techniques Study

Use the description below of this study and the data set indicated to answer the research questions listed. You will need to use both descriptive and inferential statistics to complete this project. You can download the SPSS data file Analysis_project_2.sav from http://psychology .illinoisstate.edu/jccutti/StatsDataFiles/Analysis_project_2.sav for the analyses. Write an APA-style results section based on the analyses you conducted.

Research Project Description

This study investigated the effect of teaching technique on measures of learning and interest in the topic. Two sections of a sociology course received different teaching formats. One section experienced a traditional lecture format while the second section was taught with a combination of lectures, web-based activities, and in-class exercises. Learning of the course material was measured by the grade on the final exam and interest was measured with a topical interest scale developed by the researcher.

The researchers (pretend that's you) are interested in several questions:

- Is there a difference between the two teaching formats in learning of the material?

- Is there a difference between the two teaching formats in interest in the material?

- Is learning related to interest in the topic?

Data Set Details

- **subject:** This refers to the subject number assigned to each subject. Each row corresponds to one subject's data.

- **teach:** This variable refers to which condition each subject was in (1 = lecture only, 2 = mixed).

- **learn:** This variable refers to the learning of the material.

- **interest:** This variable refers to the interest in the topic.

67. Data Analysis Project 3: Distracted Driving Study

Use the description below of this study and the data set indicated to answer the research questions listed. You will need to use both descriptive and inferential statistics to complete this project. You can download the SPSS data file Analysis_project_3.sav from http://psychology .illinoisstate.edu/jccutti/StatsDataFiles/Analysis_project_3.sav for the analyses. Write an APA-style results section based on the analyses you conducted.

Research Project Description

This study investigated the effects of distractions while driving. Participants were asked to drive a car around a test track of orange cones. Two types of distracting activities were tested: One group of drivers conducted a conversation on a cell phone while driving the course, the other group were asked to eat a Big Mac value meal (Big Mac, fries, and a drink) while driving the course. Both the average driving speed and the number of orange cones knocked over were measured.

The researchers (pretend that's you) are interested in several questions:

- Is there a difference between eating and talking on a cell phone for average speed?

- Is there a difference between eating and talking on a cell phone for the number of cones knocked over?

- Is average speed related to number of cones knocked down?

Data Set Details

- **subject:** This refers to the subject number assigned to each subject. Each row corresponds to one subject's data.

- **distrac:** This variable refers to which condition each subject was in (1 = eating, 2 = cell phone).

- **speed:** This variable refers to the average driving speed.

- **cones:** This variable refers to the total number of cones knocked over.

68. Data Analysis Project 4: Temperature and Air Quality Study

Use the description below of this study and the data set indicated to answer the research questions listed. You will need to use both descriptive and inferential statistics to complete this project. You can download the SPSS data file Analysis_project_4.sav from http://psychology.illinoisstate.edu/jccutti/StatsDataFiles/Analysis_project_4.sav for the analyses. Write an APA-style results section based on the analyses you conducted.

Research Project Description

The Environmental Protection Agency is investigating claims that global temperatures are higher and air quality is worse now than they were in 1950. They sample the temperature on a single day in several random cities. They also measure the air quality index for these cities. Data were collected in a similar manner from random cities in 1950.

   The researchers (pretend that's you) are interested in several questions:

- Is there a difference between 1950 and 2003 temperatures?

- Is there a difference between 1950 and 2003 air quality?

- Is temperature related to air quality?

Data Set Details

- **city:** This refers to the subject number assigned to each city. Each row corresponds to one city's data.

- **year:** This variable refers to which condition each subject was in (1 = 1950, 2 = 2003).

- **temp:** This variable refers to the temperature in the city when sampled.

- **quality:** This variable refers to the air quality in the city when sampled (higher scores mean better air).

69. Data Analysis Project 5: Job Type and Satisfaction Study

Use the description below of this study and the data set indicated to answer the research questions listed. You will need to use both descriptive and inferential statistics to complete this project. You can download the SPSS data file Analysis_project_5.sav from http://psychology .illinoisstate.edu/jccutti/StatsDataFiles/Analysis_project_5.sav for the analyses. Write an APA-style results section based on the analyses you conducted.

Research Project Description

This study examined the effect of job type (or status) on job satisfaction. Researchers studied two types of job satisfaction (specifically, satisfaction with pay and satisfaction with the work itself) for a group of university faculty and a group of university staff. Each group completed a questionnaire measuring their satisfaction with work and satisfaction with pay.

The researchers (pretend that's you) are interested in several questions:

- Is there a difference between faculty and staff in satisfaction with pay?

- Is there a difference between faculty and staff in satisfaction with the work itself?

- Is satisfaction with work related to satisfaction with pay?

Data Set Details

- **subject:** This refers to the subject number assigned to each subject. Each row corresponds to one subject's data.

- **status:** This variable refers to which condition each subject was in (1 = faculty, 2 = staff).

- **pay:** This variable refers to the satisfaction with pay measure (with a higher number meaning greater satisfaction).

- **work:** This variable refers to the satisfaction with work measure (with a higher number meaning greater satisfaction).

70. Data Analysis Project 6: Attractive Face Recognition Study

Use the description below of this study and the data set indicated to answer the research questions listed. You will need to use both descriptive and inferential statistics to complete this project. You can download the SPSS file Analysis_project_6.sav from http://psychology.illinoisstate.edu/jccutti/ StatsDataFiles/Analysis_project_6.sav for the analyses. Write an APA-style results section based on the analyses you conducted.

Research Project Description

This study investigated the effects of previous exposure on perceived physical attractiveness. In the first phase of the experiment, all of the participants were presented with 100 photographs of faces on a computer screen and asked to make an age estimation of each ("How old do you think this person is?"). In the second phase of the experiment, participants were again presented with photos of faces and asked to make two judgments: How attractive is this person (scale of 1 = unattractive, 7 = very attractive)? And how familiar is this person (1 = not familiar, 7 = very familiar)? For one group of participants, ten of the photos were from the original list (plus 15 photos of celebrities and 15 unemployed actors, but these photos were filler pictures and not used in the analysis of the data). For another group of participants, there were ten photos of new faces (plus the filler pictures).

The researchers (pretend that's you) are interested in several questions:

- Is there a difference in perceived attractiveness between the photos from the original list and the ten new photos?

- Is there a difference in familiarity between the photos from the original list and the ten new photos?

- Is attractiveness related to familiarity?

Data Set Details

- **subject:** This refers to the subject number assigned to each subject. Each row corresponds to one subject's data.

- **faces:** This variable refers to which condition each subject was in (1 = new faces, 2 = familiar faces).

- **attract:** This variable refers to the average attractiveness rating.

- **famil:** This variable refers to the average familiarity rating.

71. Data Analysis Project 7: Discrimination in the Workplace Study

Use the description below of this study and the data set indicated to answer the research questions listed. You will need to use both descriptive and inferential statistics to complete this project. You can download the SPSS data file Analysis_project_7.sav from http://psychology.illinoisstate.edu/jccutti/StatsDataFiles/Analysis_project_7.sav for the analyses. Write an APA style results section based on the analyses you conducted.

Research Project Description

This study investigated occurrences of discrimination in the workplace. In two different years (2014 and 2016), employees at a company were asked to report the number of incidents of discrimination they experienced at work. In the year between (2015), some employees participated in a discrimination awareness workshop. Different levels of employees were included in the study. Other demographics variables were also measured.

The researchers (pretend that's you) are interested in several questions:

- What do the distributions of discrimination reports look like across the years? Describe the distributions for discrimination in both 2014 and 2016.

- Which variables are significantly correlated with one another? Describe these relationships.

- Is there a significant change in discrimination reports from 2014 to 2016?

- Is there a significant change in discrimination reports in 2016, depending on training program?

- Is there an effect of job level on discrimination reports in 2016? Using a Tukey test, which groups are statistically different?

- Is there a significant interaction of gender and workshop participation on discrimination reports in 2016? If so, describe the interaction.

Data Set Details

- **Participation:** Some employees chose to attend the discrimination awareness workshop (1 = participated, 2 = did not participate) in 2015.

- **Gender:** This variable refers to the subject's gender (1 = female, 2 = male).

- **Age:** This is the age of the employee at the 2016 testing point.

- **Joblevel:** This variable refers to the employee's job level (1 = staff, 2 = lower management, 3 = upper management).

- **Yearscom:** This variable refers to the number of years each employee has been with the company at 2016 testing point.

- **Yearsed:** This variable refers to the number of years of post–high school education each employee has.

- **Jobsat:** This variable refers to the job satisfaction score from questionnaire (higher scores mean greater satisfaction).

- **Ethnicity:** This variable refers to each employee's self-reported ethnicity.

- **Discr2014:** This variable refers to the number of discrimination incidents reported during 2014.

- **Discr2016:** This variable refers to the number of discrimination incidents reported during 2016.

SECTION 4

How to Choose a Statistical Test

This section of the lab manual will focus on skills related to choosing the appropriate statistics to analyze a data set. It will include flowcharts to help lead students to the correct tests for different kinds of data as well as activities that ask them to actually choose the test, conduct it, and interpret the results.

72. Using the Flowchart to Find the Correct Statistical Test

Use the flowchart to answer the questions about the correct statistical test for each situation described. Indicate if there is more than one appropriate test and in which cases each test should be used.

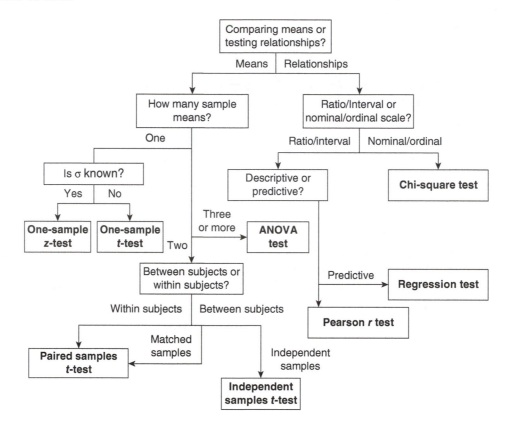

(1)   You want to describe the relationship between two measured variables.

(2)   You have a single sample that you want to compare with a population with a known mean (μ).

(3)   You have two sample means (from different groups of subjects) that you want to compare.

(4)   You want to be able to predict a score on a ratio variable from a score on an interval variable.

(5)   You have sets of twins you are comparing on a measure.

73. More Using the Flowchart to Find the Correct Statistical Test

Use the flowchart to answer the questions about the correct statistical test for each situation described. Indicate if there is more than one appropriate test and in which cases each test should be used.

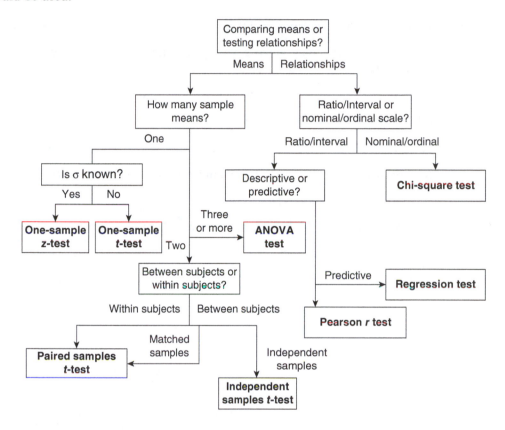

(1) A study uses a sample of dogs to compare their ability to find a buried treat before and after a training session they participate in.

(2) You want to know if students' college grade point average predicts their starting salaries in their first postgraduation job.

(3) Individuals who are right- and left-handed were recruited to compare these groups on spatial ability.

(4) After a new curriculum is implemented, the scores on a standardized test for all second graders in a school ($n = 80$) are compared to the known population mean on the test.

(5) You want to know how studying with silence, classical, or rock music in the background compare in terms of exam scores for a class.

74. Research Design Exercise

For the research questions below, describe a study to answer the question using the research design specified. Be sure to state any dependent variables in your study. State your hypothesis for your study and use the flowchart to indicate which statistical test(s) you could use to test your hypothesis.

1. Does watching violence on TV cause violent behavior? (experiment)

2. Do people who play video games have better hand–eye coordination in other tasks? (correlational)

3. Does divorce in families negatively affect children? (correlational)

4. Are smoking and lung cancer related? (quasi-experiment)

5. Does studying with background music improve test scores? (experiment)

6. Are there fewer helping behaviors in large cities? (correlational)

7. Are color and mood related? (correlational)

8. Are caffeine and work productivity related? (quasi-experiment)

9. Does watching violence on TV cause violent behavior? (correlational)

10. Do people who play video games have better hand–eye coordination in other tasks? (experiment)

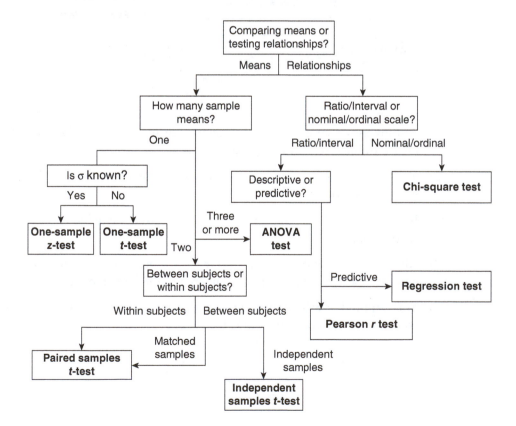

75. Design and Data Collection Exercise

For each study description below, identify the data collection technique and the research design that were used. Then use the flowchart to indicate which inferential test should be used to analyze the data for that study.

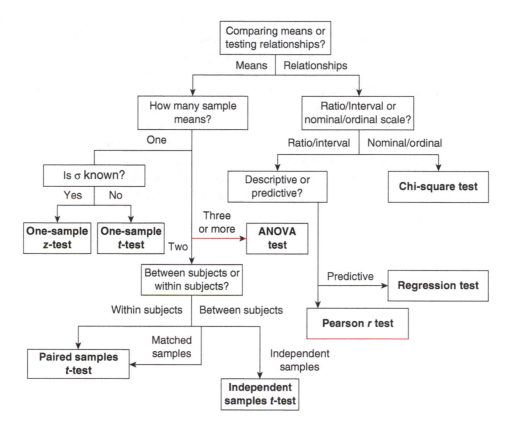

(1)   Researchers (Bartecchi et al., 2006) were interested in the effects of a new law banning smoking in public places on health. They compared heart attack rates for two cities of comparable size; one city had enacted a smoking ban one year before the study and the other city had no smoking ban. To compare heart attack rates, the researchers examined hospital records in each city. They compared heart attack rates for the year before the smoking ban in each city and for the year after the ban was enacted. They found that heart attack rates decreased in the city with ban from one year to the next but did not decrease in the city without the ban.

Data collection technique:

Research design:

Inferential test:

(2)   To evaluate the validity of a newly created survey measure of college students' satisfaction with their major, a researcher (Nauta, 2007) administered a survey to college students who had declared a major. She then also collected the students' grade point averages (GPAs) (with their permission) from the university registrar to examine the relationship between their survey score and their GPA. She found that satisfaction with major was positively correlated with GPA.

Data collection techniques (Hint: there is more than one in this study):

Research design:

Inferential test:

What does it mean that she found a positive relationship between GPA and survey score?

(3) Researchers (Assefi & Garry, 2003) were interested in the effects of the belief that one has consumed alcohol on cognition. In particular, they tested whether a belief that subjects had consumed alcohol during the study would increase their susceptibility to memory errors. Subjects were randomly assigned to one of two groups. In one group, they were told the drink they consumed had contained alcohol (with some alcohol rubbed on the outside of the glass for realism). In the other group, they were told the drink did not contain alcohol. All subjects then saw a slide show of a crime (shoplifting). After a short delay, subjects then read a description of the crime that contained errors. After another short delay, they answered questions about the slides they had seen and were asked to rate their confidence in their answers. Subjects told they drank alcohol made more errors in their answers and were more confident in their responses.

Data collection technique:

Research design:

Inferential test:

76. Designs and Analyses

For each study description below, list the relevant variables and then use the flowchart to find the correct statistical test to use and which effects will be tested in this analysis.

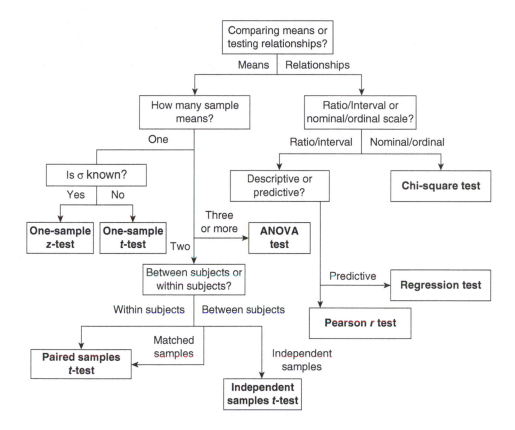

1. A psychologist is interested in the effect of peer pressure on risk-taking behaviors of college students. The psychologist designs an experiment to determine this effect: 200 students (who volunteer to serve as participants) are randomly placed in one of two situations. In each situation, five participants sit in a room with four other people. The four other people are actually confederates of the experimenter (i.e., they are part of the experiment), and their behavior is determined before the experiment begins. Half of the participants witness the four other people in the room leaning back in their chairs (a behavior that involves the minor risk of falling over backward in the chair). The other half of the participants also witness the four confederates leaning back in their chairs but are further encouraged by the confederates to exhibit the same behavior (e.g., they tell the subjects that leaning back is more comfortable, fun). The behavior of each participant is observed to determine if they do or do not lean back in their chair during the experiment. For each group, the number of participants (out of five) who lean back in their chairs is recorded.

    a. List any independent variables in this study and the levels of each one.

    b. What is the dependent variable and how is it being measured?

    c. What statistical test should be used to analyze the data from this experiment? What effects will be tested in this analysis?

2. A research methods instructor wants to know if having students conduct their own research study as part of the course increases their understanding of major concepts in the course. To investigate this, she gives two sections of her course a pretest on the course concepts. She then gives one section a research study assignment for the course but does not give this assignment to her other section. At the end of the semester, she gives a posttest to both sections on the course concepts and compares the difference in the pretest–posttest scores as a measure of learning for the two sections of her course. The section with the research study assignment shows more learning.

    a. List the quasi-independent variables in this study and the levels of each one.

    b. What is the dependent variable and how is it being measured?

    c. What statistical test should be used to analyze the data from this quasi-experiment? What effects will be tested in this analysis?

Describing and Interpreting Results in APA Style

This section will provide students with exercises to practice writing APA-style results sections from SPSS output and examples of analysis results written in APA style to help them learn how to describe results from different types of tests.

77. Writing a Results Section From SPSS Output: *t* Tests

A study was conducted in which 36 participants completed an experiment in which ads were presented subliminally during a task (e.g., Coke ads were flashed at very fast rates during movie ads). Participants were then given a recognition test for images in the ads: Two images were presented and participants had to choose which one of the two was presented earlier. However, the researcher wanted to know if standard ads (e.g., a glass of Coke is being poured over ice) were remembered differently than emotional ads (e.g., a person drinking a Coke is tightly hugging another person). To test this, each of the 36 participants completed the recognition task for both types of ads (i.e., when first presented, both types of ads were shown in a random order and recognition trials were included for both types of ads). Thus, each participant had a separate recognition score for standard and emotional ads.

The SPSS output for this study appears below. Use the output to write an APA-style results section for this study.

t Test

Paired Samples Statistics

		Mean	*N*	Std. Deviation	Std. Error Mean
Pair 1	Standard Ads	53.5000	10	10.40566	3.29056
	Emotional Ads	66.3000	10	12.68464	4.01123

Paired Samples Correlations

		N	Correlation	Sig.
Pair 1	Standard Ads and Emotional Ads	10	.118	.745

Paired Samples Test

		Paired Differences							
					95% Confidence Interval of the Difference				
		Mean	Std. Deviation	Std. Error Mean	Lower	Upper	*t*	*df*	Sig. (2-tailed)
Pair 1	Standard Ads and Emotional Ads	−12.800	15.42581	4.87807	−23.835	−1.7650	−2.624	9	.028

78. Writing a Results Section From SPSS Output: ANOVA

A study was conducted to examine the effect text format has on student satisfaction for two subject topics: chemistry and psychology. Text format was manipulated across student groups with paper text, standard electronic text, and an interactive electronic text. Students taking either introductory chemistry or introductory psychology courses were recruited as participants in the study. Their satisfaction with the assigned text was measured at the end of the course on a scale of 1 to 10.

The SPSS output for this study appears below. Use the output to write an APA-style results section for this study.

➡ **Univariate Analysis of Variance**

[DataSet0] /Users/dmmcbri/Documents/Stats Text/Lab Manual/xercise_78.sav

Between-Subjects Factors

		Value Label	N
Type of Text	1.00	Paper	40
	2.00	Standard Electronic	40
	3.00	Interactive Electronic	40
Subject Topic	1.00	Psychology	62
	2.00	Chemistry	58

Descriptive Statistics

Dependent Variable: Student Satisfaction Rating

Type of Text	Subject Topic	Mean	Std. Deviation	N
Paper	Psychology	4.8500	1.63111	20
	Chemistry	5.0000	1.55597	20
	Total	4.9250	1.57525	40
Standard Electronic	Psychology	5.2500	1.64845	24
	Chemistry	5.1875	2.00728	16
	Total	5.2250	1.77573	40
Interactive Electronic	Psychology	7.8333	1.94785	18
	Chemistry	7.4545	1.71067	22
	Total	7.6250	1.80721	40
Total	Psychology	5.8710	2.13083	62
	Chemistry	5.9828	2.07315	58
	Total	5.9250	2.09506	120

Tests of Between-Subjects Effects

Dependent Variable: Student Satisfaction Rating

Source	Type III Sum of Squares	df	Mean Square	F	Sig.	Partial Eta Squared
Corrected Model	176.883[a]	5	35.377	11.675	.000	.339
Intercept	4147.129	1	4147.129	1368.602	.000	.923
text	176.154	2	88.077	29.066	.000	.338
topic	.278	1	.278	.092	.763	.001
text * topic	1.408	2	.704	.232	.793	.004
Error	345.442	114	3.030			
Total	4735.000	120				
Corrected Total	522.325	119				

a. R Squared = .339 (Adjusted R Squared = .310)

Estimated Marginal Means

1. Type of Text

Estimates

Dependent Variable: Student Satisfaction Rating

Type of Text	Mean	Std. Error	95% Confidence Interval	
			Lower Bound	Upper Bound
Paper	4.925	.275	4.380	5.470
Standard Electronic	5.219	.281	4.662	5.775
Interactive Electronic	7.644	.277	7.096	8.192

Pairwise Comparisons

Dependent Variable: Student Satisfaction Rating

(I) Type of Text	(J) Type of Text	Mean Difference (I–J)	Std. Error	Sig.[b]	95% Confidence Interval for Difference[b]	
					Lower Bound	Upper Bound
Paper	Standard Electronic	-.294	.393	1.000	-1.249	.662
	Interactive Electronic	-2.719[*]	.390	.000	-3.667	-1.771
Standard Electronic	Paper	.294	.393	1.000	-.662	1.249
	Interactive Electronic	-2.425[*]	.394	.000	-3.383	-1.467
Interactive Electronic	Paper	2.719[*]	.390	.000	1.771	3.667
	Standard Electronic	2.425[*]	.394	.000	1.467	3.383

Based on estimated marginal means

*. The mean difference is significant at the

b. Adjustment for multiple comparisons: Bonferroni.

79. Interpreting Results Exercise:
Sproesser, Schupp, and Renner (2014)

The researchers in this study were interested in how social situations can influence stress-induced eating. They grouped subjects according to self-reported stress-induced eating habits: consistently eating more (hyperphagics) or less (hypophagics) when stressed. Each subject was then exposed to one of three social situations: (1) a social inclusion condition in which subjects were told that a confederate partner had approved of a video they had made answering some questions and was looking forward to meeting them, (2) a neutral condition in which they were told their partner could not meet them because they had to cancel their participation, or (3) a social exclusion condition in which they were told that their partner had decided not to meet them after viewing their video. Subjects were then given an ice cream taste test and the amount of ice cream consumed was measured.

A portion of the results section from this article appears below. Using the study summary above, describe what the results for this study mean in your own words.

> We conducted an analysis of variance (ANOVA) with condition (social inclusion, social exclusion, neutral) and eating style (stress hyperphagia, stress hypophagia) as independent variables and food consumption in grams as the dependent variable. The main effects were not significant, which indicates that neither condition (exclusion: $M = 108$ g, $SE = 9.6$; neutral: $M = 112$ g, $SE = 7.9$; inclusion: $M = 120$ g, $SE = 8.5$), $F(2, 135) = 0.11$, $p = .893$, nor eating style (stress hyperphagics: $M = 119$ g, $SE = 9.1$; stress hypophagics: $M = 110$ g, $SE = 5.9$), $F(1, 135) = 0.47$, $p = .493$, affected food intake during the taste test. However, as predicted, a significant Condition × Eating Style interaction emerged, $F(2, 135) = 7.71$, $p = .001$. In the neutral condition, both stress hyper- and hypophagics consumed a comparable amount of ice cream; hyperphagics consumed a mean of 111 g ($SE = 14.1$), and hypophagics consumed a mean of 112 g ($SE = 9.6$), $F(1, 135) = 0.01$, $p = .928$. As expected, in the social-exclusion condition, stress hyperphagics ate significantly more ice cream ($M = 147$ g, $SE = 13.7$) than did stress hypophagics ($M = 86$ g, $SE = 10.5$), $F(1, 135) = 12.40$, $p = .001$. The mean difference of 61 g between the two types of eaters corresponds to a difference of 120 kcal. Conversely, in the social-inclusion condition, a reversed pattern emerged: Stress hyperphagics ate significantly less ice cream ($M = 92$ g, $SE = 16.3$) than did stress hypophagics ($M = 130$ g, $SE = 10.0$), $F(1, 135) = 3.95$, $p = .049$, a difference of approximately 74 kcal.

80. Interpreting Results Exercise: Ravizza, Uitvlugt, and Fenn (2017)

The researchers in this study were interested in the relationship between Internet use during class and learning. The participants in the study logged in to an Internet server during class on their laptops; the researchers monitored the time spent online and the type of site (academic and nonacademic) that the students viewed during class time. They also measured the students' scores on the cumulative final exam in the class, ACT scores, and interest in the course material.

A portion of the results section from this article appears below. Using the study summary above, describe what the results for this study mean in your own words.

> Nonacademic Internet use, composite ACT scores, motivation to do well, and interest in the class were all significant predictors of the score on the cumulative final exam (Table 2). Academic Internet use was not related to final exam score, $r(82) = .09$, $p = .43$. Neither ACT scores nor motivation was significantly related to laptop Internet use for class-related or non-class-related purposes. Interest in the class approached significance, $r(76) = -.19$, $p = .096$; that is, there was a trend for greater interest in the class to be related to lower laptop Internet use for nonacademic purposes. Motivation and interest were also related such that greater interest in the class material predicted higher motivation to do well.

Table 2   Correlations Among Cumulative Final Exam Score, Actual Internet Use, Composite ACT Score, Motivation to Do Well in Class, and Interest in Class

Variable	Actual Academic Internet Use	Actual Nonacademic Internet Use	ACT Score	Motivation	Interest
Final Exam Score	0.09	−0.25*	0.36*	0.33*	0.26*
Interest	0.09	−0.19†	−0.10	0.43*	–
Motivation	0.15	0.01	0.00	–	
ACT Score	−0.06	0.07	–		

†$p < 0.10$

*$p < 0.05$

Appendix
Summary of Formulae

Univariate Statistics	For a Population	For a Sample
Mean	$\mu = \sum \dfrac{X}{N}$	$\overline{X} = \sum \dfrac{X}{N}$
Sum of squares	$SS = \sum (X - \mu)^2$	$SS = \sum (X - \overline{X})^2$
Variance	$\sigma^2 = \dfrac{SS}{N}$	$s^2 = \dfrac{SS}{n-1}$
Standard deviation	$\sigma = \sqrt{\sigma^2} = \sqrt{\dfrac{SS}{N}}$	$s = \sqrt{s^2} = \sqrt{\dfrac{SS}{n-1}}$
z score	$z = \dfrac{X - \mu}{\sigma}$	$z = \dfrac{X - \overline{X}}{s}$

Bivariate Statistics

Sum of the products $SP = \sum (X - \overline{X})(Y - \overline{Y})$

Pearson r correlation coefficient $r = \dfrac{SP}{\sqrt{SS_X SS_Y}} \quad \dfrac{\sum z_x z_y}{n-1}$

Degrees of freedom $df = n - 2$

Regression line $\hat{Y} = (X)(\text{slope}) + (\text{intercept}) = Xb + a = bX + a$

Slope $b = \dfrac{SP}{SS_X}$

Intercept $a = \overline{Y} - b\overline{X}$

Total squared error $SS = (Y - \hat{Y})^2$

Standard error of estimate $s_{est} = \sqrt{\dfrac{SS_{error}}{df}}$

Hypothesis Testing and Parameter Estimation

z Test

Standard error (σ known) $\sigma_{\overline{X}} = \dfrac{\sigma}{\sqrt{n}}$

z observed $z_{\overline{X}} = \dfrac{\overline{X} - \mu}{\sigma_{\overline{X}}}$

Effect size $d = \dfrac{\overline{X} - \mu}{\sigma}$

Parameter estimate (σ known) $\mu = \overline{X} \pm z_{crit}(\sigma_{\overline{X}})$

One-Sample t Test

Degrees of freedom $n - 1$

Standard error (σ unknown) $s_{\overline{X}} = \dfrac{s}{\sqrt{n}}$

One-sample t observed $t = \dfrac{\overline{X} - \mu}{s_{\overline{X}}}$

Effect size $d = \dfrac{\overline{X} - \mu}{s}$

Parameter estimate (σ unknown) $\mu = \overline{X} \pm t_{crit}(s_{\overline{X}})$

Related-Samples t Test

Degrees of freedom $n_D - 1$

Mean of differences $\overline{D} = \dfrac{\Sigma D}{n}$

Sum of squares of differences $SS_D = \Sigma(D - \overline{D})^2$

Standard deviation of differences $s_D = \sqrt{\dfrac{SS_D}{n_D - 1}}$

Standard error of differences $s_{\overline{D}} = \dfrac{s_D}{\sqrt{n_D}}$

Related samples observed t $t_{\overline{D}} = \dfrac{\overline{D} - \mu_{\overline{D}}}{s_{\overline{D}}}$

Effect size $d = \dfrac{\overline{D}}{s_D}$

Parameter estimate (related samples) $\mu_D = \overline{D} \pm t_{crit}(s_{\overline{D}})$

Independent Samples t Test

Degrees of freedom $df_1 = (n_1 - 1), df_2 = (n_2 - 1)$

$$df_{total} = df_1 + df_2 = n_1 + n_2 - 2$$

Pooled variance of independent samples $s_p^2 = \dfrac{SS_1 + SS_2}{df_1 + df_2}$ $s_p^2 = \dfrac{s_1^2 + s_2^2}{2}$

(2nd averaging formulas if $n_1 = n_2$)

Standard error of independent samples $s_{(\overline{X}_1 - \overline{X}_2)} = \sqrt{\dfrac{s_p^2}{n_1} + \dfrac{s_p^2}{n_1}}$ $s_{(\overline{X}_1 - \overline{X}_2)} = \sqrt{\dfrac{2s_p^2}{n}} = s_p\sqrt{\dfrac{2}{n}}$

(2nd formula if $n_1 = n_2$)

Independent samples observed t $t_{obs} = \dfrac{(\overline{X}_1 - \overline{X}_2) - (\mu_1 - \mu_2)}{s_{(\overline{X}_1 - \overline{X}_2)}}$ =

Effect size $d = \dfrac{\overline{X}_2 - \overline{X}_1}{s_p}$

Parameter (independent samples) $\mu_1 - \mu_2 = \overline{X}_1 - \overline{X}_2 \pm t_{crit}(s_{(X_1 - X_2)})$

Chi-Square Test

Estimated cell frequencies $f_e = \dfrac{f_{column} f_{row}}{n}$ or $f_e = \dfrac{f_{row}}{n} * f_{column}$

Observed chi-square $x^2 = \sum \dfrac{(f_0 - f_e)^2}{f_e}$

Degrees of freedom $df = (\#columns - 1)*(\#rows - 1)$

References

Assefi, S. L., & Garry, M. (2003). Absolut memory distortions: Alcohol placebos influence the misinformation effect. *Psychological Science, 14,* 77–80.

Bartecchi, C., Aldever, R. N., Nevin-Woods, C., Thomas, W. M., Estacio, R. M., Bartelson, B. B., & Krantz, M. J. (2006). Reduction in the incidence of acute myocardial infarction associated with a citywide smoking ordinance. *Circulation, 114,* 1490–1496.

Nairne, J. S., Pandeirada, J. N. S., & Thompson, S. R. (2008). Adaptive memory: The comparative value of survival processing. *Psychological Science, 19,* 176–180.

Nauta, M. M. (2007). Assessing college students' satisfaction with their academic majors. *Journal of Career Assessment, 15,* 446–462.

Ravizza, S. M., Uitvlugt, M. G., & Fenn, K. M. (2017). Logged in and zoned out: How laptop Internet use relates to classroom learning. *Psychological Science, 28,* 171–180.

Sproesser, G., Schupp, H. T., & Renner, B. (2014). The bright side of stress-induced eating: Eating more when stressed but less when pleased. *Psychological Science, 25,* 58–65.

von Hippel, W., Ronay, R., Baker, E., Kjelsaas, K., & Murphy, S. C. (2016). Quick thinkers are smooth talkers: Mental speed facilitates charisma. *Psychological Science, 27,* 119–122. doi: 10.1177/0956797615616255